VOLUME

4

Rental Property Management Basic Training

REAL ESTATE INVESTING

Library of Congress -in-Publication Data
March 2003
Txu-1-204-543
Real Estate Investing Rental Property Management Basic Training

10 9 8 7 6 5 4 3 2 1

The enclosed material is designed for educational purposes only. Each State may have different certification and specific guidelines. Please refer to your State for additional and future information. The information contained herein is considered correct at the time of creation but laws and regulations are updated frequently and the reader assumes the responsibility for confirming current regulations and applicable data. The publisher and author make no warranty as to the success of the individuals using the training material contained herein. The publisher and author make no warranty as to any action taken by any individual completing this program. The reader is responsible for the appropriate use of the materials and information provided. This publication is designed to provide accurate and authoritative information concerning the subject matter. All material is sold with the understanding that neither the author nor the publisher guarantees the actions of any individual making use of the inclusions. Neither the author nor the publisher is rendering a legal opinion, accounting recommendation or other professional service. If legal advice or other expert assistance is desired, the services of a legal professional or other individual should be sought. The applicable federally released forms, disclosures and notices are generated from public domain. Copyright law does apply to all intellectual materials and all rights under said law are reserved b y the copyright owner.

Coursework is available at special quantity discounts to use as premiums and sales promotions within corporate or private training programs. To obtain information or inquire about availability please write to Director, PO Box 1, Hollidaysburg, PA 16648.

RENTAL PROPERTY MANAGEMENT
BASIC TRAINING

HISTORY AND OVERVIEW 1

In the 1920's a virtual boom in the need for multi-family buildings occurred. At that time, the actual property owner managed most residential-rentals. Because of the rapid growth in residential rental real estate, many owners relied heavily on bank funds to expand and build their rental unit ownership to a level that met the new demand for multi-family housing. This expansion allowed a higher income to act as a means of support for the owner. When the great depression occurred, the banks foreclosed on many of these heavily mortgaged properties.

Banks were not then, and are not today, in the business of managing properties. Because the banks interest in the foreclosed buildings had to be maintained in the form of value retention, the banks looked for property managers to take over the care of these properties.

This need created a new career opportunity in America. In 1933 the Institute of Real Estate Management was formed. This group was initially comprised of responsible Real Estate Management firms. Each member firm was required to adhere to certain bylaws and pledges.

The firms were required to keep a separate bank account for each client and not to co-mingle client's funds.

They were also required to keep fidelity on employees and not to benefit from client profits without providing full disclosure.

In 1938, the Institute of Real Estate Management converted its membership to include individuals. After this conversion the title and designation of Certified Property Manager was created. To obtain this designation an individual was required to meet certain requirements. These requirements have carried through to present time.

Designation requirements include

The need to manage 300 units of residential rental property, not individual buildings but the units contained in the buildings.

A requirement to complete required course work or study

The ability to draft and submit a management plan to the Institute of Real Estate Management

Despite the existence of large property management firms, many rental property owners, especially those with a smaller rental portfolio, were forced to either manage their property or seek out individual property managers to oversee their investments.

Those individuals who do not meet the professional property management designation often took residential property management positions that enabled them to live at a greatly reduced cost while earning an income overseeing the rental property.

Today, both firms and individuals take an active part in the management of multi-family residential real estate rentals. Each of these may obtain a specific designation showing their background and expertise in the field. The Institute of Real Estate Management continues to oversee the designations, as do individual States.

Today's economic environment has again created a situation that includes a rise in foreclosed property, an increased demand for short term housing units, and individuals relocating to other regions of the country who are in need of rental property for housing both short and long term. This new boom in real estate rental housing has increased the demand for both professional and private real estate rental property managers.

Gaining a solid understanding of the fundamentals of rental property management is the first step toward successfully managing your own real estate investment portfolio or entering the field of a professional real estate property manager with more knowledge, tools, and skills than 95% of your competing managers.

Whether you are seeking the knowledge you need to manage your own real estate investment portfolio, gain the skills you need to become a resident property manager or obtain the fundamental knowledge needed to decide if a career as a certified property manager is for you, it is important to understand the different property-management designations.

Certified Property Manager

An individual may still obtain the designation of Certified Property Manager through the completion of required education, the building of a portfolio of managed units and by adhering to the codes required for a certified property manager. Today's codes are similar to the codes originally established in 1933 and involve using fair and ethical practices in your dealings with the public.

Accredited Resident Manager

Individuals may obtain an additional designation. This designation is Accredited Resident Manager. This designation requires coursework similar in nature to that of the Certified Property Manager but provides a variation on the units managed requirement numbers. A resident manager is required to live on site at the property they are managing.

Certified Property Management Firm

A firm may obtain the designation of Certified Property Management Firm by meeting a few simple criteria. They are required to employee at least one full time Certified Property Manager on staff and provide fee for management services for their clients without conflict of interest.

Investment Property Manager

An Investment Property Manager's job is to manage every aspect of the operations and property activity to create the highest possible financial return for the investor.

The manager's functions may include

Renting apartment units

Performing all service relations with the tenants

Completing or overseeing building renovations and repair

The supervision of maintenance personnel

Accounting

Advertising

Report preparation

Property managers usually receive a salary plus a bonus for meeting certain goals such as occupancy ratios.

To be a successful property manager, one must have the ability to combine the skills of public relations and marketing expert, complete advanced bookkeeping tasks, remain in control of but at ease with the tenants all while overseeing renovation personnel completing tasks on the property.

The fees paid to an investment property manager will typically be set in one of three formats.

- A manager may charge a percentage of the gross rents received.

- A manager may receive a percentage of the net operating income obtained.

- A manager may perform the functions negotiated with the property owner for a set fee regardless of rents received or not received.

The composition of gross rents and net operating income are explained in some detail in a later chapter. For the present, it is enough to proceed with a basic understanding of the fees available for charge.

A residential property manager will typically be compensated in part through the offset of the rental fee for the unit they occupy and then receive a smaller fee per unit payment for the balance of their income.

The career of professional real estate management will be composed of many facets. Some of the functions required for effective property management include

- Leasing

- Marketing

- Community outreach

- Maintenance

A property management firm or individual may contract to complete some or all of these tasks. Some property management firms employ different individuals, each of whom specialize in only one facet of the property management process. In some cases, one fully trained and multi-faceted individual completes all of the tasks. The versatility involved in customizing job function requirements is a negotiation point when contracting with a property owner. An individual who is going to specialize at specific sub-functions within the general property management structure will typically have a different title than simply property manager. These titles will vary slightly by region or by specific property owner.

Before beginning the process of choosing the position, you wish to fill within a management firm or the services you wish to offer to a property owner, it is important to understand the duties inherent in each position title.

General Property Manager

Perhaps the most common position in any real estate rental management firm is that of General Property Manager. The General Property Manager will be responsible for between 2 and 20 rental buildings containing a variety of rental units. The General Property Manager will often oversee the performance of any Resident Managers employed by the firm and are typically the supervisors of the Leasing Consultant and Leasing Consultants. Another function often performed by the General Property Manager is the creation and implementation of budgets for all rental buildings.

In some firms, it is common practice for the General Property Manager to perform many of the job functions outlined under the titles Leasing Consultant and Marketing Specialist.

Depending on the size and structure of the firm, the functions of these positions may be assigned to specific individuals with specialized skills in particular areas. These specific individuals will be responsible for the completion of only one facet of the firms business and are therefore obtain specific experiences or skill sets than those provided by a more generalized position.

A firm that employees a specially trained individual for each task may be an excellent opportunity for a beginning property managers. This type of employer allows you to focus more fully on obtaining the knowledge and skills of the position you fill without the distraction of a more diverse set of duties.

An individual who chooses to follow this path may find it beneficial to perform the tasks of one position until the desired level of expertise has been obtained. You can then request a lateral career move to another position. This ability to focus on one piece of the overall function at a time provides a stronger knowledge base if the employee wishes to one day begin their own firm or to acquire residential rental properties of their own.

On the other hand, obtaining the position of General Property Manager who completes a more diverse group of tasks in relationship to the property will allow the individual to gain skill at all of the functions of property management. This creates a situation where the individual can experience all of the facets of the field during a relatively short time.

Experiencing all of the different facets of the career gives the individual an excellent opportunity to determine exactly what functions best suit their particular skill set and which functions will require enhanced education. By gaining a diverse skill set, a property manager can also maintain as broad a career path giving them more diversity and career options in the future.

Executive Property Manager

The top of the property rental hierarchy in most Real Estate Management firms will be the position of Executive Property Manager. The owner of the management firm usually performs the duties of the Executive Property Manager but this may be a position that is staffed.

The Executive Property Manager is the one who will plan and oversee all facets of the business and will bear the ultimate responsibility for all activities taken by the firm and its employees. In many instances, it will also be the responsibility of the Executive Property Manager to seek out new clients or rental buildings to manage.

The Executive Property Manager may perform marketing activities in an attempt to secure a higher ratio of rented units. These functions may be shared with a Director of Marketing or a Leasing Consultant. In addition, the Executive Property Manager will be responsible for all staffing needs of the firm, for the ultimate planning and approval of all budgets and for the profit and loss of the firm as well as its individual client buildings.

Marketing Specialist

A firm may contain a Marketing Specialist whose job function is to market each of the managed properties. These marketing efforts are geared toward the goal of establishing a strong rental ratio for the managed properties. Without rented units, none of the other activities of the firm is necessary.

The primary goal of any property owner, property manager or firm is to rent the units available.

Without tenants who pay rent, none of the other people involved in real estate, rental management can be successful.

It is the function of the Marketing Specialist to ensure that enough rental applications are generated through their marketing efforts to enable the units to be rented to solid, dependable tenants. The ultimate goal of the Marketing Specialist is to maintain a high occupancy ratio of good quality tenants helping to ensure the continued profitability of the rental unit under management.

Leasing Consultant

The position of Marketing Specialist will sometimes be combined with that of the Leasing Consultant. A Leasing Consultant is an individual licensed to negotiate lease terms.

The primary task of the Leasing Consultants is to handle the showing of rental units, negotiate lease terms, and oversee the collection of rents. In some firms, the Leasing Consultant will also help to format the standard lease offered for the property and create special lease promotions that draw potential tenants to the property.

It is often the role of the Leasing Consultant to provide work orders for and oversee work activity of the maintenance personnel.

The Leasing Consultant will also be in charge either solely or in conjunction with the Marketing Specialist, of Community Outreach Programs. These community outreach programs enable to the management firm to play a strong role in the community and in aiding individuals who would otherwise have difficulty finding suitable housing in securing rental units.

Leasing Consultants are typically the front line people in any firm and therefore must have excellent customer service skills. They will handle most of the contact with the public in showing rental units, negotiating lease terms, collecting rental payments and dealing with rental issues.

Resident Property Manager

A property owner that requires a more direct approach to property protection, site maintenance, and tenant oversight will often retain the services of a Resident Property Manager. The services offered by a Resident Property Manager will be specific to the needs of the property but will usually encompass many of the tasks offered by a general property manager.

The Resident Property Manager typically receives compensation in a manner similar to other property managers but the exact percentage of cash payment will traditionally be less than the payment to property managers who live off site. The remaining compensation is in the form of free or reduced housing within a unit at the property.

In exchange for the compensation benefit of reduced cost or even free housing, the Resident Property Manager will often assume additional duties and responsibilities beyond those expected of a general property manager. In many cases, the Resident Property Manager will oversee the daily operations of the rental unit, oversee maintenance personnel or even perform maintenance tasks themselves, and act as a front line person with the public. The activities with the public will often include the showing of rental units to prospective tenants, the collection of rental payments, and the negotiation of leases and oversight of the security of the units.

In larger complexes, the Resident Property Manager may have help in the completion of these tasks through the hiring of a non-resident employee who will perform one or a combination of the tasks normally completed by the Resident Property Manager. In most cases, the Resident Property Manager will perform any task that is necessary to keep the property secure, in good condition, and filled with quality tenants.

The tasks involved in residential rental real estate management vary and encompass a wide array of job tasks. This is a multi-faceted field with a broad range of duties. The owner or firm with which you work may require a person to complete some or all of the tasks outlined.

Beyond the specific positions are sub-functions that must be accomplished in order to manage a residential investment property.

Administrative Functions

Administrative tasks are often assigned on a strength basis to a variety of individuals within a firm. An individual Property Manager will need to become adept at completing all of the administrative functions or find a reliable outsourcing partner to complete these functions on their behalf.

The administrative tasks vary and cross over nearly every portion of property management. They are grouped in function as they all pertain to the completion of records for the property.

The administration portion of the property management position entails the maintenance of property accounting through either a manual or computer created system. The purpose is to record all activity of the property including rent collections and deposits, move-ins, move-outs, returned checks, security deposits, vendor income and miscellaneous income of the property.

It is often a task of the administrator to make delinquency reports; monthly cash receipt summaries and perform any other accounting reports necessary to keep the owner or firm manager informed of financial activity of the property. The specific reporting requirements for the rental property will be outlined by the property owner or within the firm's policies and procedures handbook.

The administrator will collect rent payments from tenants, send late notices in the event of a late payment and deliver notices to quit premises as well as filing said notices with the proper judicial authority. The person who is assigned these duties will also typically represent the owner or firm in hearings that result from these complaints. This person will also be responsible for collection of past due accounts or act as a liaison with collection agencies in the event the account collection becomes an issue outside their scope.

The administration duties also encompass tracking records such as the maintenance of tenant files to ensure that they include all information pertaining to the leases, renewals, maintenance request, notice to and from tenants, correspondence and other information that is deemed important.

The firm or property owner may require a variety of reports. It is typically the duty of the administrator to complete and provide these reports for review. This needed information may pertain to vacancy reports, monthly management reports and any other information that may be needed to keep the owner or management firm informed about the operations and activity of the property.

The administrator will prepare also budget projections and may have the authority to purchase goods and services necessary for the operation of the property. They will also review monthly accounting statements and analyze variance by line item between budget expectations and actual income/expense results.

Leasing Functions

The primary task of any property owner or management firm is to lease units. The property management firm or a member of the property management team will be required to execute lease agreements and renewals on behalf of the owner or company.

The individual assigned the leasing functions will need to show apartments to prospective tenants and to aide in establishing marketing strategies and plans.

The individual who is completing the leasing functions will often set up a system of communication with competitive property owners or management staff to aid in obtaining knowledge of the operations and success ratio of the direct competition.

Leasing functions also include the tracking of all move-ins and move-outs including property inspections, repair, restoration, and decoration of the units as well as the processing of the security deposit refund forms.

Operations/Maintenance

Preparations and maintenance functions may fall under any job description within a management firm but there are often tasks that are specifically included in the category of Maintenance.

The primary maintenance activity is to inspect the buildings and grounds of property or complex and report deficiencies. Often the same person who completes the inspection will act to correct the problems. These acts may be to correct the problem themselves or they may require the submission of a cost analysis of the deficiency as well as a working plan as to how the deficiency will be corrected to the property owner or firm manager.

The maintenance function will often obtain estimates for major repairs or improvements from licensed contractors and submit these estimates to the owner or manager for approval.

The individual assigned to complete the operations or maintenance tasks should also study ways to improve contracted services such as trash removal, air-conditioning, exterminating and laundry services as well as any other service provided at the property to help increase the value of the services offered to the tenants and to increase the profitability of the rental property.

Personnel Office

The personal office or director will hire employees, maintain employee payroll files, and keep time records. The personnel director typically trains the administrative staff, provides operational overview of office functions and reviews and evaluates employee performance. The personnel director will schedule training programs and interact with the staff to provide open communication. One goal of the personnel director is to stimulate the staff to generate new ideas and solve problems.

Whether you work for a property management firm, for yourself or in another capacity, a contract with the owner of the property is an important facet to understanding your duties and obligations to the owner. A clearly defined contract ensures the owner of the property to whom you offer your services understands the limitations and parameters of your offerings.

A sample Property Management Agreement is included on the following pages for you review. This form is for example and educational purposes only. You should always retain the services of a real estate professional in the creation of any contract.

The Landlord-Owner

The landlord-owner is an integral part of your property management team. Whatever your position, it is the efforts of this individual that has created the opportunity for you to achieve success. The landlord-owner will review the bottom line results of every individual on the property management team to determine the future efforts that must be made to retain profits and increase the potential of the property you are managing.

The landlord-owner typically reviews all of the reports provided by every member of the management team to determine how the efforts you put forth meet the goals he established at the time he purchased the investment property.

The vital factor to remember is that the profitability of the rental property is ultimately the only goal of the landlord-owner. You and other members of the management team will handle the day-to-day operations activity. The landlord-owner will make the final determinations as to what renovations, repairs, upgrades and even the decision on the continued operations.

The last chapters of the coursework provide you with the financial data that a landlord-owner must review before any decision regarding any recommendations you make can be made.

Career Goals

The career opportunities in the field of property management are varied. Once you have obtained a strong knowledge of property management and an understanding of the marketing requirements and the numbers necessary to achieve profitability, the ability to enter this field successfully will be within your grasp.

- You can start your own property management firm, making it as large or as small as you desire.

- You can become an on-staff property manager, marketing specialist or leasing consultant for an established firm in your area.

- You can obtain a position as a resident manager, which will allow you to obtain a paycheck for your efforts and reduced or even free housing within the rental building or complex.

- You can take your personal knowledge and skills and combine them with the strong knowledge base you are building to create a customized position that suits your specific needs and skills.

As you read through and learn the materials included you will see that the Property Management career option offers a variety of facets and career opportunities.

Each of these options provides obvious opportunities but each also carries responsibilities.

You will want to review the overview of responsibilities for different titles to begin planning what path your career may take.

You will plan exactly how you can obtain a career that will fulfill your personal needs while providing an excellent position with fantastic career benefits.

You might even plan how you will structure your own firm to obtain a fantastic income while maintaining the independence of being your own boss and owning a business of your own.

It is important that you gain a comprehensive understanding of the stability and growth offered by your new career choice.

Investing in real estate is the most profitable and stable growth opportunity available to today's investors.

Vacant property and bank maintained units are growing at an enormous pace offering job growth potential unsurpassed in other industry options.

Investment real estate has the potential to provide a higher growth margin than nearly any other investment opportunity. Investment real estate has consistently shown itself to be a stable arena that continues to prosper, despite shifts in economic conditions, alterations in housing prices, job markets or any other outside factor.

The one factor that will most dramatically influence the potential that real estate investment offers to the investor and to those who make their careers handling these investments is the preparation and understanding with which each investment property is managed.

Well-trained property managers are essential to the profitability of any real estate investment property.

Upon completion of this course, you will have gained a comprehensive understanding of the management techniques necessary to manage an investment property at a profit.

Residential real estate investment is the most common opportunity you will encounter when you first begin in the field of property management. The samples and examples we will review will emphasize the management of residential real estate but the tools you will learn can be applied to any type of real estate investment you will encounter. It is vital that you understand the actions you must complete not only from a career perspective but also from the viewpoint of the investor for whom you will be working. The investor has chosen real estate as the best growth opportunity for his portfolio and it will be an essential part of your role to ensure that the investor achieves the expected returns. The more profitable the investment is for the investor, the more stable and satisfying your position will be.

PROPERTY MANAGEMENT AGREEMENT

This Agreement is made and entered into this _____ day of
_____, 20_____ between _____
(Owner) and _____ (Manager).
Owner employs the services of Manager to manage, operate, control, rent and lease the following described property: _____
_____.

1.   **Responsibilities of Manager**
      Owner hereby appoints Manager as his lawful agent and attorney-in-fact with full authority to do any and all lawful things necessary for the fulfillment of this Agreement, including the following:

A.   *Collection and Disbursement*
      Manager agrees to collect all rents as they become due; to render to Owner a monthly accounting of rents received and expenses paid; and to remit to Owner all income, less any sums paid out. Manager agrees to collect the rents from the tenant and to disburse funds by ordinary mail or as instructed by the Owner on or before the 10th day of the current month, provided, however, that the rent has been received from the tenant.

B.   *Maintenance and Labor*
      Manager agrees to decorate, to maintain, and to repair the property and to hire and to supervise all employees and other needed labor.

16

C.   *Advertisement and Legal Proceedings*
Manager agrees to advertise for tenants, screen tenants and select tenants of suitable credit worthiness. Manager will set rents that in the opinion of the Manager at the time of the rent negotiations with the tenant reflect the market conditions of that time. The manager will approximate rents of comparable rental properties, unless expressly instructed in writing by the Owner to the Manager to the contrary. The manager will document the amount of the initial rent and any subsequent increases as may from time to time be appropriate. Manager agrees to rent and to lease the property; to sign, renew and to cancel rental agreements and leases for the property or any part thereof; to sue and recover for rent and for loss or damage to any part of the property and/or furnishings thereof; and, when expedient, to compromise, settle and release any such legal proceedings or lawsuits.

2.   **Liability of Manager**
Owner hereby agrees to hold Manager harmless from, and to defend Manager against, any and all claims, charges, debts, demands and lawsuits. Owner agrees to pay Manager's attorney fees related to Manager's management of the herein-described property and any liability for injury on or about the property, which may be suffered, by any employee, tenant or guest upon the property. Owner agrees to maintain sufficient and prudent all risks property insurance and that the Manager shall be an additionally named insured. Owner shall provide a copy of such insurance policy to the Manager for the Manager's records.

3.   **Compensation of Manager**
Owner agrees to compensate Manager as follows.

Owner agrees to pay the Manager an amount equal to fifty (50%) percent of the first full month's rent as a fee for acquiring, screening, and renting the premises; and further agrees to ten (10%) percent of all rents collected, (minimum

$40.00 per month), as a fee for managing the property; which fees, plus any repair expenses, may be deducted by the Manager from rents, and further agrees to abide by the conditions set forth by the Manager to the tenant on the Owner's behalf.

4.   **Term of Agreement**
This Agreement shall be effective as of the _____ day of _____, 20____ and shall expire on the _____ day of _____, 20____.

Upon expiration of the above initial term, this Agreement shall automatically be renewed and extended for a like period of time unless terminated in writing by either party by providing written notice _____ days prior to the date for such renewal.

This Agreement may also be terminated by mutual agreement of the parties at any time.

Upon termination Owner shall pay to Manager any fees, commissions and expenses due Manager under terms of this Agreement, which are owing to Manager.

In the event of the premises not renting within a 90-day period of entering into this agreement, or of a vacancy continuing for a period of longer than 90 days, Owner reserves the right to declare this agreement void

5.   **Successors and Assigns**
This Agreement shall be binding upon and inure to the benefit of the successors and assigns of Manager and the heirs, administrators, successors, and assigns of the Owner.

Notwithstanding the preceding sentence, Manager shall not assign its interest under this Agreement except in connection with the sale of all or substantially all of the assets of its business. In case of such sale, Manger shall be released from all liability under this Agreement upon the express assumption of such liability by its assignee.

This document represents the entire Agreement between the parties hereto.

IN WITNESS WHEREOF, the parties hereto hereby execute this Agreement on the date written above.

_____

_____
Owner   Manager

Figure 1:1   Sample Property Management Contract

MARKETING

2

The first and primary goal of any person involved in residential real estate property management is to keep the properties rented. The rental payments will fund all other actions from paying the employees to providing income for the property owner. In general, the obtainment of rental payments is the sole purpose of property management.

Many property managers do not consider themselves salespeople. However, without marketing and sales skills, you cannot perform any other portion of your job function. You must master the basic marketing and sales skills that will allow you to rent the property units that you have available. These sales skills will enhance your ability to secure the best tenants by generating interest in the property you have available to every prospect. By generating interest the unit to each prospect, you will ensure that you have a stronger pool of candidates from which to choose your tenants and that the vacancy ratio for the property you manage is lower than that of competing properties.

If the units you have available are vacant, they are not generating income. Through exceptional marketing and sales skills, you can minimize these vacancies and therefore increase the income and profits the property will generate.

The first step to becoming an exceptional property manager is to obtain the educational base you will need to perform well in your new career.

The second step is to fine-tune your marketing and sales skills.

Simply explained marketing is the act of notifying the targeted client base those goods or services are available and moving those goods or services to the consumer.

The explanation of marketing sounds simple but the execution of marketing tasks can be quite complex. The following pages are designed to give you a basic overview of marketing and the efforts you can take which will allow you to secure lease contracts.

Establish a Target Market

The first step in marketing is to establish your target market.

You must know whom you intend to reach with your marketing efforts before you can begin to create and implement a marketing plan.

In residential real estate rentals, your ultimate goal will be to reach people desiring a residential rental unit. There are various categories where you may find the prospective tenants.

Many Property Managers find it easy to decide whom they wish to target but forget the need to know why these targets desire rental housing.

If you do not know the stimuli behind these groups decision to obtain rental housing, you will not be able to adequately market to these individuals.

The most common people who desire rental housing and will be your targets are:

- Single individuals

- Young un-married couples who share housing

- Young married couples

- Family groups including children

- Empty-nesters

- Retired individuals

All of these groups will be looking to establish housing.

Each of these groups will have a different goal in mind for their household and it is your job to help emphasize the features that make the housing units you have available an excellent choice to meet their housing goals.

The first three groups of people will have little or no experience in renting or setting up their households. Your goal with these individuals will be to act as a mentor making the establishment of their household very easy and the process convenient.

The next primary group will be families who have chosen not to purchase a residence.

These families will be looking for children friendly housing that provides enough space for their family and a safe environment in which to raise their children.

To target this prospective tenant group you will want to create a community atmosphere that is kid friendly and provides the necessary space for active and growing family units.

Another key group of renters, which is becoming more prominent in today's society, is the "empty nesters" or people whose children have grown.

These people will often find they have too much space and responsibility as homeowners and decide to rent.

This particular group will be looking for suitable housing that requires minimal upkeep and maintenance on their part.

You will want to emphasize the ease of living at your complex or building to target this group.

The housing units you manage may not be suitable for every target market. You should spend some time viewing the units, the grounds, and the surrounding community from the perspective of the potential tenants. Make yourself a list of features, amenities, and benefits that you can refer to for each particular subgroup of prospective tenants.

Once you have determined the people who will comprise your target market and how your rental units can meet the needs of the target market, you must plan how you will let them know that you have rental units available to suit their needs.

Before you ever begin reviewing the potential locations of your advertisements, you must compare your available units with the competition. Any factor that makes your offerings more desirable than those offered by the competition will be an essential component in creating an advertisement that gets attention. Some items you might focus on would include:

- Number of Bedroom

- Convenient Locations

- Security

- Specialized heating or air conditioning systems

- Types of closet and storage

- Community features such as clubhouse or gated entry

- Availability of town resources such as schools or shopping

- Interesting Floor Plans

- Any additional feature that sets your unit apart and above the competition

You should begin the marketing process by identifying:

- The three most competitive features offered by your unit or community

- The benefits the tenant will obtain from these features

- The way your unit can save the tenant money or increase their comfort

A tenant, like any individual on the other side of the sales process is interested in the concept of "what is in it for me".

One of the most essential factors that assist a successful salesperson is to remember to discuss only those items that are important to the prospect.

A potential tenant is not interested in what you will achieve through the rental but rather what they will obtain by choosing to rent from you.

Planning a Marketing Strategy

Marketing is as important to the career of a successful property management as training, knowledge, talent, or the property you are representing.

Marketing encompasses any action that creates a prospective tenant or generates inquiries for the property manager.

A property manager who cannot competently market for prospective tenant leads and lease applications will quickly find that no matter their background, education, desire or skill level, they will not succeed in this business.

Your income as a property manager is often directly related to how many lease applications you can bring across your desk and turn into rented units. Many property managers make the mistake of assuming marketing is incidental to the overall picture. They assume if they learn to operate in their chosen profession in a competent and service oriented manner the referrals will follow. These same property managers are still sitting at their desk waiting for the telephone to ring or are now in a different profession.

The second mistake a property manager may make with marketing efforts is to assume that the same flier and advertising campaign all of their competitors are using is an adequate method of marketing. The reality is that the market has seen these letters, fliers, and advertisements many times and they have lost a great deal of their effectiveness.

The materials contained in this program are designed to aid you in preparing your own marketing efforts and understanding the reasoning behind each task a successful property management professional will perform.

We have included items which are copy and go or in which you can insert your logos, work with a printing service or alter the text when necessary. These materials will guide you through your first year, but will also offer you the opportunity to become one of the few property managers who is capable of developing and implementing a marketing program of their own.

An essential task, before you begin marketing for prospective tenants, is developing a system for tracking the effect of your marketing efforts. Early in your career, the balance of your time will be spent marketing including making contacts, building relationships, getting your name and that of your chosen rental complex out to your target groups. This abundance of available time gives you the opportunity to experiment. You will be able to use a variety of options to determine what works best for you.

Each person's strengths and weaknesses are different and therefore each person's marketing plan should be different.

As you build your business as a property manager, you will need to begin redirecting your efforts to negotiation and processing of leases. At that time, it will become very important to expend your marketing efforts in the areas that bring you the strongest return. To determine where your valuable time and energies should be expended you will need solid market penetration figures. As time management becomes vital to your continued success, these figures will allow you to determine, based on solid tracking numbers, exactly what provides success for you!

The Phone-Query Questionnaire included later in the course is an excellent and time efficient method of tracking. Providing you have asked each referral how they heard about you, these forms, easily bound in a binder for quick access, will give you an excellent overview of what marketing efforts have yielded a return.

Another method of tracking referrals and marketing penetration figures is to use a Database Management system. ACT! or another similar system will allow you to track your marketing efforts, prepare reports, and maintain all contact information and documentation and to minimize the paper requirements of your office.

Experiment with different methods of tracking your success to find the tracking system that will work best for you. Just be sure you HAVE a system.

Whatever method of tracking you use, knowing what brings in the clients and what does not is well worth the time involved in creating and utilizing the tracking plan.

Marketing Schedule and Strategy

Before you begin to market for tenant applications, you must develop a schedule and strategy.

Early in your career, you will spend the balance of your time marketing. You must get your name out there in front of the referral sources, the potential clients and the affinity service providers.

The more your name and face are in front of all of these people the more quickly they will give you the opportunity to work on an application for and with them.

Each person's strengths and weaknesses are different and therefore their marketing plan should be different.

Many marketing programs you will see assume that each property managers will follow the same marketing pathways. This error in thought has caused more than one potentially successful property manager to leave rental management for another career.

The information contained in this program offers you many ideas and options to choose from when beginning or continuing your marketing efforts. It is up to you to experiment and determine what will be effective for you and your particular market.

When deciding where to begin your marketing efforts you must remember that you do not want to duplicate the over-used efforts of you competitors. You will want to focus on important marketing arenas your competitors are forgetting.

The first step to creating your plan is to create a schedule. A schedule will help keep your marketing efforts moving in the correct direction and keep you from inadvertently pushing marketing to the back burner.

Begin by reading this entire program. While you read, you should make careful notes to aid you in determining which efforts you would like to implement first.

Upon completion of this coursework, purchase a day planner that allows you to allocate each day's working time into fifteen-minute increments.

The first entries into your day planner should be broad entries.

If you are working for a property management firm, you will want to check with your supervisor to determine what, if any, continued education they are planning to provide for you.

If you have chosen to enter the property management business as an independent manager, it is even more vital that you plan your continued training with an eye toward becoming one of the more professional managers in your area.

Many experienced property managers believe that continued education is not important to their success. They tend to believe that by actually performing the job, they are succeeding in staying abreast of industry changes and have all of the knowledge they need to continue to succeed.

It is important to remember that property management is a professional career opportunity and should be treated as such. No matter what your success level or how many years you have logged, you must continue your education to ensure that you remain the most knowledgeable and professional manager in your region.

Many professions have continuing education requirements to ensure that the already well skilled individuals performing in the business hone their skills and remain knowledgeable about every industry change. Leasing does not have such a firm requirement in many states, but you should act as if the industry has these continuing education guidelines in place.

Making room in your marketing plan for enhanced learning will ensure that once you gain the reputation as the best in the industry and that you remain a top performing property manager for the life of your career.

Enter the dates and times for your continuing education into the specific time-allocation slots on your day planner.

The next entries should be broad tasks you plan to complete each day.

Make sure you do not over-schedule your day.

You will want to vary your tasks so that you are not attempting to spend an entire workday out, in the public, making sales calls or conversely the entire day behind your desk working on paper. You may eventually wish to time block tasks of a specific type but early in your career each workday should contain a time block for each type of task on your task list to ensure that you get everything done.

To plan all of your sales calls in the same day can also be self-defeating. It is virtually impossible to make call after call and remain fresh and excited.

The fresher you are when you approach a prospective referral source, the better the impression you will make on that individual.

A sample task list might appear something like this

	Monday	Tuesday	Wednesday	Thursday	Friday
	Advertising Research	Referral Calls	Investor Guidelines	Referral Calls	Place Advertisements
8:00	Call ------ Newspaper For pricing	Copy Handouts	Review Products from _____ Investor	Copy Handouts	Call --------- Newspaper to place ad.
8:15	Call ------ magazine for pricing	Begin calls at ------- Referral	Continued Review of guidelines	Begin calls at --- ----- Referral	Call ------ magazine to place ad

The first step in generating a master schedule is to list all of the broad category tasks you expect to accomplish such as advertising research, telephone contacts, continued education, and sales calls.

As you can see, this schedule contains a simplified entry for each day's efforts that lists just one broad item. The example schedules first entry is Advertising Research. The research functions are then broken down into smaller tasks. Time blocking a certain period for research is an excellent organization decision but to say you are going to accomplish research today is a broad item. You should break the broad goal down to specific tasks such as call newspapers for pricing, call magazines for pricing, etc.

Broad category entries allow you to set aside time blocks for a particular type of task. Segmenting the broad item into time specific smaller tasks allows you to maintain an effective use of your time.

The schedule included in this package is a sample for training purposes. You will base your initial marketing plan upon your strengths and specific market conditions. We used the tasks listed as examples because they are tasks you will undoubtedly accomplish during your first weeks in the field.

The timing of the tasks on your list is also very important. You will want to make telephone calls at a time that you are more likely to find someone in the office, like early in the morning rather than a time when people are traditionally away from their desks, like lunchtime.

Sales calls should occur at a time that is convenient to the person on whom you are calling. You should also plan your sales calls around your natural rhythms in terms of energy levels. Some people are more social in the morning while others find they feel more social in the afternoon. You would want to plan face-to-face calls at the time that is best for you.

The same process of considering the timing of an activity holds true no matter what the task. Whether you are making calls, studying materials, writing advertisements or even reviewing application packages you should remember that each person is different and therefore his or her daily schedule of tasks should vary accordingly.

Goal Setting

Marketing involves one other very important activity. You must set realistic and achievable goals in order to effectively schedule and complete the tasks included in your marketing strategy.

Goals must meet some general criteria:

Visible

Your goals should be visible to you. The first thing you should do when attempting to complete a group of tasks is to create a list of your goals.

The master task list ensures you can see each short-term goal you have set for yourself. Keeping goals in a prominent location will allow you to keep your focus in place.

Realistic

Realism is a very important factor when setting your goals.

Setting goals unrealistically high will cause feelings of failure and discouragement.

Each time you carry these feelings away from your day it becomes more difficult to approach the next day's task list with enthusiasm, interest and drive.

Setting goals unrealistically low may cause initial feelings of success, but will eventually cause you to stagnate.

Achieving goals that are set too low will cause you to feel a false sense of accomplishment and cause you to minimize your future efforts.

Without realistic goals, you will never develop your business to the level of success you desire.

Time Oriented

An important part of goal setting and task management is to allow a sufficient amount of time for the completion of the task and the attainment of your goal.

If you do not incorporate enough time in your schedule to accomplish each goal, you will place unnecessary pressure on your shoulders.

You will not accomplish the tasks you set out for yourself and you will foster a feeling of failure.

Allowing a sufficient amount of time for each goal will promote attention to detail and positive reinforcement.

Broken Down

Goals should be broken into the smallest parts.

You may have a general overview of a project or task and all of the parts you must accomplish in your head, but you should make the effort to write each part on your task list.

You must view these parts as separate tasks.

Listing each component of a goal separately allows you to schedule and accomplish each step in the best order.

Breaking goals into the smallest parts also ensures you do not overlook an essential step in the process. Overlooking essential steps often leads to a crisis. An integral part of your marketing-management plan is to minimize the time invested in crisis activity.

Short Term and Long Term

Goals should also be set that are short term and that are long term.

The shorter the time frames of your goal the more of a priority level it receives.

If you do not list both short and long term goals, you will minimize the benefits of excess schedule time.

Maximizing excess time in your schedule ensures that you work ahead and use every minute available in your workday.

Short-term goals provide a sense of urgency that will stimulate you to accomplish the tasks on your schedule each day.

Long-term goals provide a sense of working ahead that stimulates your sense of control.

Working on tasks well before they become a high-priority task allows you to pace your schedule and ensure you retain the ability to complete each task before it is due.

Choosing Marketing Areas

There are six beginning marketing options with proven results for a Property Manager.

- Print Advertising

- Direct Mail

- Signs/Billboards

- Community Outreach

- Sales Presentations

- Direct Referrals/Networking

Your market plan may contain only a couple of these options or a combination of all of these options. You will need to balance your

- Strengths

- Budget

- Market conditions

- Time

To determine how you wish to attack your particular market.

Advertising

Before beginning to consider advertising as an effective source of potential tenant referrals, you will need to understand the regulations concerning advertising practices.

There has been a lot of confusion concerning advertising practices. This confusion centers on the exact terms and phrases that can and cannot be included in an advertisement.

The confusion concerns words and phrases that may be construed as discriminatory.

The phrase master bedroom may seem an ideal method of describing one of the many features of your apartment unit, but it could be considered a discriminatory phrase in certain parts of the country.

HUD has taken on the task of determining exactly what can and cannot be used as advertising for the Real Estate Community.

You should check any phrase the might be questionable through HUD before printing your advertisement. Sometimes the change of a simple word or two can make all of the difference to how your advertisement is viewed. The regulations allow a broad array of options with relatively easy guidelines. In effect, you simply must use caution when composing your advertising so as not to include any item that may be considered discriminatory in nature.

HUD has stated that newspapers cannot be held liable for the words they print in conjunction with real estate advertising.

It is the responsibility of the advertiser to phrase their offerings in such a way that they are not offensive to any individual or group.

The Federal Fair Housing Act prohibits the use of discriminatory advertising or advertisements that state a preference for a particular type of person.

You may not advertise in a manner meant to attract or deter a potential client based on race, color, religion, sex, handicap, familial status or national origin.

Spend some time on the HUD website before composing any advertising. Sometimes the words chosen for an advertisement can look dramatically different when they are viewed from the perspective of another person.

It seems like stating that a unit has great views or is near amenities would be a common practice when advertising an available rental but if you select certain phrases those same features can become a discriminatory act. When advertising, the following phrases are allowed and not considered as discriminatory for handicapped individuals:

Great View   Jogger trails
Walk up   Walk to bus stop
Walk in Closets

Handicapped individuals are to have the same benefit of enjoyment as any other prospective tenant.

You must make the ability to modify the property in a reasonable manner available to any individual with a handicap.

These modifications cannot be done in a manner that interferes with the reasonable enjoyment of any other occupant and the modifications are to be at the expense of the individual.

You should include a disclaimer that the complex or rental agent "does not discriminate on the basis of race, color, religion, national origin, sex, handicap or familial status" if you have any doubts as to the wording of your advertisement. This will not offset a blatant act of discrimination but may help to cover you in the event you use a word or phrase that is within the gray area.

HUD has available an entire listing of specific guidelines for your review. The nature of advertising allows you a broad spectrum in which to operate. It is important to remember that discrimination in real estate practice is illegal. Providing you are not targeting particular strata of society for either positive or negative staying within the guidelines is relatively easy.

Planning the Advertising Campaign

Your first goal with an advertising campaign is exposure. Unless your target market knows who you are, where you are and what you can do for them, they will never call!

Print Media and Radio Media are the two most common forms of advertising for property rentals.

Radio & television advertisements are designed to promote name recognition.

Print advertisements are designed to convey information.

As a beginning property manager, you will probably want to focus on print and leave the more costly radio advertising to your firm location. If you budget allows for radio advertising, then you should certainly consider adding it to your campaign if you feel it is beneficial but most investment property managers need to be concerned with the bottom line and print is traditionally less costly than radio or television.

Print advertisements will build name recognition in the market place and you will build personal recognition just not as quickly as with a radio or television campaign.

Many newspapers offer a free "new in business" mini-article. This is a brief blurb telling the public

- That you are now in business

- Who you are

- Your specialty

- Where you can be contacted

This is an excellent first step in getting your name out there. Best of all it is typically free. Some newspapers offer this mini-article with a small photograph of you. It is important to have this professional photograph available before contacting the newspaper about this opportunity. This advertisement should not be confused with the "Welcome Aboard" paid advertisement you may run. This article is typically a human-interest piece published free by the newspaper.

Many firms, no matter their advertising budget are willing to place a "Welcome Aboard" advertisement notifying the public that they have a new Property Management Specialist available.

Check with your supervisor to see if this is a common practice. If not, research pricing and write your own advertisement. Often, when approached with a completed package your supervisor will rubber-stamp his or her approval on the advertisement. Exposure for you is exposure for the firm!

The following advertisement is an excellent new Property Management Specialist announcement. Remove the underlined sections and insert your information in the area provided.

<u>Company Name</u>
is proud to Welcome <u>Your Name</u>
a certified Property Management Specialist.

Specializing in <u>Your Property Specialty</u>
Homes, <u>Your Name</u> is available to provide
FREE information and showings!

Give <u>Your First Name</u> a call today and welcome him/her aboard! <u>Telephone Number</u>

You will note the advertisement gives:

- Your company (where you are)

- Your name (who you are)

- Your title (showing your capabilities)

- Your specialty (notifying your target market that you are here FOR them)

- A FREE offer (nothing will make your phone ring faster than the word FREE!)

- An order to call today (people sometimes need permission to call)

- Instructions on how and when to contact you

If you are able to place an advertisement specific to you, you will want to make every dollar count. Research ALL of the print media in your area.

Primary newspapers, Real Estate Guides, Apartment Magazines, Bargain Shopper Style Newspapers and anything else specific to your region are excellent beginnings to your research

You will want to determine the target market and circulation of each media forum and compare how that market relates to your target market.

The cost of advertising in each form should be considered against the potential gain you may obtain.

You should also spend some time assessing where other property management firms are finding success with their advertising efforts.

Once you have these figures, arrange a meeting with your firm manager to determine exactly what the firm is willing to fund for you.

Once you know what you can spend, make the final decision as to where you wish to place your advertising. You should weigh the cost of the advertisement against the circulation and market of each media source. You should quickly determine that one or two options outstrip the competition.

Now it is time to begin your advertisement campaign. You will want your advertisement to be understandable, efficient and direct. In addition, bear in mind, when composing the advertisement, the majority of the population comprehends at no more than an 8th grade reading level.

People also remember because of repetition.

You will want to vary your advertisements to a degree, but you will also want to repeat advertisements to achieve the repetition and familiarity that causes your target market to remember your advertisement and take action.

All advertisements should be composed so that they contain the same general combination of items.

- The advertisement should contain an attention getting header gets the attention of the reader within your target market.

- The advertisement should include questions that are actually the most common excuses for why people do not call a property manager.

- The advertisement should have a strong statement reassuring your reader that you can answer their questions. Something as simple as I CAN HELP is usually sufficient.

- Each advertisement should give the reader permission to call you while stressing that the consultation is absolutely FREE. Many people cannot resist free especially when it is tied to something they truly want, a new home.

- The advertisements should be short (therefore less costly), concise, and simple to understand.

An advertisement that contains all of these bulleted points just like the new in business announcement example should make your phone begin to ring very quickly as long as you have correctly identified the best media for your target market and included the information your target market needs to want to make the call.

Shorter, more concise advertisements are more appropriate for a newspaper source or billboards.

Longer, advertisements that are more detailed are useful with less costly print media like an Apartment Guide.

These keys to advertisement composition are effective in any form of print advertisements. These components should be included whether you are creating an advertisement that will be placed in a print media source, a flier that will be placed in common areas that your target groups can be depended upon to enter, or another venue specific to your area.

Group Presentations

When you have a specific feature or amenity available at your rental property that will be beneficial to a specific group, you may wish to hold a group meeting to highlight the benefits of your available units. Examples of times you might give a group presentation would be if you have a rental property that you manage that caters to the college student market or if you have a rental property near a hospital that would be suitable for hospital staff.

Group presentations can be an excellent opportunity to allow a specific target market to get to know you and to gain an understanding of the benefits and features of your rental property. Some people do not give group presentations because of fear. The most common fear that people have is the fear of public speaking. Whether you are addressing a group of one or two individuals with whom you are very familiar or addressing an assembly there are some basic actions you can take to reduce your self-consciousness and increase your confidence. We will review some basic presentation skills that you should implement and practice.

To make a winning presentation you must prepare. Preparing means that you should know the subject matter you must discuss, feel confidence in your abilities to inform and relax, because the audiences for your presentation are people just like you.

Meeting Preparation

There are preparatory tasks you can complete to reduce your internal tension when presenting an agenda.

1. Know the agenda.

   Each meeting or presentation has certain goals that the meeting must address.

   Preparing an agenda that incorporates all of these goals will allow you to maintain a consistent flow during the presentation without forgetting any of the vital points you needed to cover.

   Having a tight agenda gives you control of the meeting. You will be able to minimize outside discussions and address all essential materials simply by following your own agenda.

2. Research the topics.

   If you are giving a joint presentation, you should know who is to present what materials during the meeting, who will answer questions, and how the presentations will be ordered. You will also want to research each partner's portion of the presentation in case something goes wrong. This allows you to step into your partners place and give their portion of the speech if necessary.

3. Memorize your opening.

   The most difficult task of public speaking is to begin. Once you start your presentation, your preparation will enable you to relax into the flow of your agenda.

   Before entering the meeting or presentation always review the first few sentences of your agenda or speech so that they will flow naturally off your tongue. Once you have made it through the first few sentences, you will find that your knowledge of the agenda and preparation allow the remainder of the meeting to flow smoothly.

4. Take a deep breath.

   Before entering the meeting, you should spend a few seconds performing a deep breathing exercise.

Inhale slowly through your nose.

Hold the breath for a few seconds.

Exhale slowly through your mouth.

Repeat this process until your nervous tension begins to dissipate.

   The focus you place on the breathing exercise will reduce your ability to focus on the performance you must give.

   Deep breathing reduces nervous tension and supplies additional oxygen flow to your body providing greater relaxation.

Taking a deep breath before entering the room will enable you to begin speaking with few pauses. This ensures a flow and confidence to your opening statements that will capture the attention of your audience and enhance your feelings of confidence.

Taking a deep breath before speaking adds depth and power to your voice. A deep and powerful voice projects confidence and gains attention. This will assist you in maintaining the attention of the audience. If you do not have an adequate air supply, your voice will sound weak and mousy. A weak, mousy voice shows a lack of confidence. It will cause your audience to lose interest.

5. Speak slowly and clearly.

    A slow, well-modulated voice will project an aura of confidence that causes your audience to listen more closely to what you are saying.

    Later we will tell you to vary your pace and your pitch to emphasize important points but you should always return to a slow, clear and well-modulated tone to ensure you project confidence to your listeners.

    Speaking too quickly and allowing your words to run together shows your nervousness and causes your audience to strain to understand what you are saying.

6. Smile before you begin speaking.

    You convey the expression on your face in your voice.

    A smile on your face and in your voice serves to relax both you and your audience.

    Entering the room and beginning your discussion with a smile will generate a relaxed feeling and enthusiastic response from your audience and in your own mind.

7. Present the appropriate appearance.

   Confidence is linked to how other people view you. It is difficult to project confidence if your appearance is not appropriate. Others base their decisions concerning your abilities and character on the appearance you present to the world. Most people will form their opinions of you within the first thirty seconds of meeting you.

   Knowing you present the appropriate appearance to the world and project the impression you desire, will go a long way toward building your confidence and reducing the nervousness you feel in-group situations.

The Presentation

You have learned how to adequately prepare for a presentation, take steps to ensure you present a confident and professional appearance and plan ahead to reduce you nerves.

The following tips are items you should incorporate into the presentation itself.

Mastering presentation skills will assist you in giving a presentation that accomplishes all of your goals.

- Think of a presentation as a performance.

  While you might want to entertain, motivate and inspire your audience all at the same time, you should consider which your primary objective is and never lose focus. A good performer entertains; a great entertainer draws the audience into their world.

- Follow the agenda.

The time and attention you devote to creating and researching the topics and goals of the meeting will assist you in maintaining control and flow throughout your presentation.

- From the moment you begin a presentation, grab your audience.

  Do not give your audience the opportunity to lose interest. Grab them from the beginning with a statement that conveys why they, not you, need know this information.

- Smile with your face and your voice.

  The attitude you project as the meeting leader will set the tone for each person in the room. Smiling with your face and your voice relaxes both you and your audience and sets a positive, friendly tone for the meeting.

- Engage your audience throughout the presentation.

  Most presentations are boring. Keep the presentation moving along and engaging to make your audience more responsive.

- Make eye contact with your audience – even before you begin to speak.

  Eye contact gives each member of your audience the knowledge that they are important and stimulates attention and interaction.

- Keep your presentations moving

  State the focus.

  Hit them with the facts on the important focus or goal of the project or task.

  Finish the presentation and adjourn.

  Most presentations fail because the speaker tries to include too much information.

- Use a strong speaking voice.

  Even if you feel uncomfortable, a strong tone will inspire confidence.

  A mousy tone will cause your audience to lose interest.

- DO NOT wiggle, rock or pace.

  Transfer excess energy to your voice, expression and hands.

- Control your desire to rush.

  Slow down.

  Use pauses.

  Let the audience into your presentation.

- Vary your tempo and pitch.

  Changes in tempo help an audience maintain interest.

  Emphasize what is important by saying it more slowly and more loudly.

  You should speak points of lesser importance more softly and more quickly.

- Do not forget to "close" your presentation.

  Review the important points of the meeting from your agenda.

  Follow your close with a thanks and farewells.

  End the meeting decisively.

This shows respect for each attendee's time and leaves the participants with the feeling that the meeting provided true value.

Resist the urge to stay and chat.

After each presentation, you will need to assess your performance to determine if there are areas that need improvement. No matter how well planned and scripted, a presentation is only as effective as the performer delivering the information.

Sales Call/Presentation Critique

Preparation/ Organization	Was the planning logical and well prepared?
Style	Do your overall mannerisms enhance the quality of the call or become a distraction?
	Are dress, posture, grooming, tone and inflection appropriate for the setting?
	Can the smile be "heard" in your voice?
Use of Sales Aids	Do you explain sales aids properly?
	Are the sales aids applicable and pertinent?
	Do the sales aids add value to your presentation or are they a "crutch?"

Rapport Building	Do you create a relaxed, friendly atmosphere within the first few seconds?
Opening Statement	Do you transition smoothly to the sales portion of your presentation? Do you state an assumed need followed by a general benefit?
Active Listening	Do you pay attention to your audience? Do you appropriately paraphrase and feedback the audience objections and concerns? Do you use sentence stems such as "If I understand you..." or "So what you are saying is..."
Sell Benefits	Do you emphasize benefits rather than just features?
Product Knowledge	Do you know and articulate product features?
Managing Objections	Do you rephrase objections to clarify? Do you probe behind an objection for the real concern?

Close	Did your close include a summary of benefits?
	Did your close ask for a commitment from your audience?
Sensitivity	Did you sense your audience's emotions?
	Did you remain within the time allocated?
Control	Did you dominate and interrupt?
	Did you maintain control and keep conversation for wandering?
Verbal Expression	Were you Monotone?
	Too Loud?
	Did you use buzzwords?
Tenacity	Did you show leadership of the presentation?
Enthusiasm	Did you communicate excitement and a sense of urgency?
Confidence and Composure	Did you maintain eye contact?
	Were your facial expressions appropriate?
	Did you become rattled when pressed on a particular point?

Strategy	Were the objections raised realistic?
	Did you anticipate objections?
	Did you handle the objections appropriately?

When creating presentations it is important to establish the goals of your audience. You would not give the same presentation to an elderly person as you would at a young family seminar.

The key to each presentation is what you can do FOR THEM.

Affinity Group Marketing

Another successful technique for marketing is to network with affinity groups. Affinity groups are individuals who have contact with the same client base you are attempting to obtain but offer a different service to this group.

These affinity groups can include people such as area employers, doctors, churches and assistance agencies among others.

All of these groups have one thing in common; they have contact with the prospective tenants that you wish to secure for your property or complex but typically do not provide the same services you wish to offer.

To secure referrals from these people you will want to create a strong referral relationship with them. In order for these referral partners to feel comfortable sending prospective clients to you, they must feel that the client will be treated in a professional and service oriented manner. You and your property must be able to offer a benefit to the prospective client.

A key method of relaying vital information to these referral sources is to start an actual flier/brochure campaign. You should develop a brochure that captures their attention and promotes your services. You could show: your unit's floor plans, directions or a map to the building or complex and outlines the key features and amenities that may be of interest to the referral sources clients. Always hand-deliver these brochures and fliers

Each time you make a personal contact with the referral source you create another opportunity to impress upon that source what a professional and customer service oriented provider you are for their referrals. You also show what an exceptional job you will do with each prospective client referral they send you.

Remember by sending a prospective client to you they are putting their reputation as a good judge of character on the line with that prospect!

TELEPHONE SKILLS & PRE-QUALIFICATION

4

After you have planned and implemented your marketing strategy, the prospects will begin to arrive.

A prospect is simply a potential tenant.

The first contact from a potential tenant will often be by telephone. The purpose of the call in the prospect mind is to eliminate your units as potential housing. The reality is there are many rental units available and the tenant will begin their home search by ruling out those that are not suited to their needs.

Each time the phone rings your goal is to generate interest on the part of the caller and to secure an appointment. The first question many prospects will ask is price.

The first rule of thumb to remember is that you are selling a service as well as renting property. You must create an environment with this phone call that will allow your prospect to view you as better than your competition. You want to create interest and commitment in your caller.

The simplest method to obtain a perceived commitment on the part of the tenant is to secure as much information as possible concerning the needs of the tenant. Any piece of information you can secure allows you to customize the "pitch" to the prospect's actual situation and needs. From the moment you first speak with a prospective tenant, you should be gathering information and planning how you will negotiate the lease.

Many Property Managers fail to achieve their goals for the simple reason that they are afraid to ask for information. Information is your most valuable tool in planning a leasing sales strategy. Obtaining information is actually quite simple if you just get over the natural shyness of asking strangers for personal information. You will find that, as a professional, people will answer almost any question you ask. However, you must ask!

On the next page, you will find a "Phone-Query Questionnaire" that we recommend using for each prospective tenant. If you have this form handy, preferably bound in a notebook, you will always be able to lead the conversation exactly where you, as the Specialist, need it to go.

The pre-application questionnaire is your most important ally. Most of the information that is required in planning a leasing sales strategy is included in the questionnaire. In fact, much of the basic information that will be required for your basic lease application is included. This allows you to pre-fill some information, subject to verification during the application interview. Pre-filling saves time and allows you and the client to focus on the rental options available.

Once you have increased your business to the point that you have hired a leasing assistant, this questionnaire is a task that may be turned over to him or her for completion. It is important to note that the initial contact sets the tone for your entire relationship with these clients. Many Property Management specialists find that they prefer to complete this questionnaire with their clients themselves because there is a great deal of information conveyed that aids in the tenant placement.

The pre-application questionnaire also acts as a script to help you keep the conversation moving in the direction you need it to go. The questionnaire will allow you to handle rental inquiries in a professional and fluid manner that will reduce the fumbling and missed information that can occur during prospect tenant interviews. Even the most experienced property managers occasionally miss information and this questionnaire allows you to maintain a level of organization that will aid you in continued success.

Eventually you will become so fluid in your approach that you will not need to refer to the scripting but you will always want to have the pre-qualification questionnaire readily available.

Pre-Application Questionnaire Date: _____

Referral Source: _____

Home Phone: _____ Other Phone: _____ Best time to call: _____

Applicant Name: _____ Co-Applicant Name: _____

DOB: _____ SSN: _____ DOB: _____ SSN: _____

May I run a credit report?___ Yes ___ No   May I run a credit report? ___ Yes ___ No

Employer: _____   Employer: _____

Address: _____   Address: _____

Phone: _____ No yrs. __ Position: _____   Phone: _____ No yrs. __ Position: _____

Current Address: _____

Landlord/Mortgage Holder: _____ Phone: _____

Rent _ Own _ No. Yrs: ___ Do you know the type of apt you desire? _ Yes _ No Rent $_____

Who will be living in the home? Adults_____Children_____

Are there any special features you want? _____

_____

When will you be moving? _____

When are you hoping to secure the apartment? _____

Explanation of Special Situation/Notes: _____

_____

_____

Outcome:

Taken By: _____
L/C: _____

Pre-application questionnaire key

Date	You will always want to date the query. At times, a query will need to be 'shelved' until an issue has seasoned.	It is our recommendation that you bind each month's questionnaires in a master folder for tracking of referral sources. You will also want to keep a copy of any query that does not lead to a full application for follow-up marketing.
Referral	You will want to have this information available for informational follow-up if there is a referral partner involved with the customers. Tracking this information will allow you to assess you marketing and advertising effectiveness .	As your business grows you will find that the referral sources are more frequently word of mouth or customer referrals
Applicant's Name	You will need the applicant's full name including middle initial and any additional information Jr., Sr., II. Do not use nicknames, however please note any aliases that the borrower commonly uses.	Names, especially among family, can be very similar. The more identifying information you can acquire the more pure your credit report will be.
Co-Applicant's Name	In many instances, you will not have a co-applicant.	If the co-applicant's information is not readily available at the time of the

	When you do, it is as important to acquire correct identifying information for this person as it is for your borrower.	call, complete the primary applicant's information and request they telephone you later the same day with the co-applicant's information.
Date of Birth/Social Security Number	This information is important for the lease application and vital when you are pulling a credit report.	Always run credit reports separately. Even if the applicant and co-applicant are married, you will want to have separate reports.
May I run a credit report?	It is imperative that you ask this question. You are not allowed to run a credit report on any individual without their prior consent.	The applicant must sign credit consent forms before you run the report.
Employer	This information aids you in determining some of the issues that may arise during the course of the application.	If there is a history of job changes or there is not 2 years employment history, these will be red flags to you.
Number of years at present employment	You are looking for a minimum of two years employment history. If the applicant/co-applicant has not been in their current employment two years, you will need to trace back under comments until you have acquired a complete two-year history.	Employment stability is an excellent place to refer to when you have a lease application that requires an exception. A common compensating factor is 'at current employment more than 5 years'.

Current Address	This is identifying information you will want to have to clarify identity on the credit report.	
Landlord/Mortgage Holder	It is important to determine from the start if they pay an entity or an individual or have any previous rental history.	
Rent/Own	This question begins to draw a picture of the possible reasoning behind the prospects desire to rent.	You will customize your sales pitch to the applicants around their reasons for renting rather than your reasons for having available units.
Number of years?	You will need a two-year residence history for each applicant on the applications. If they have been at their current residence less than two years, you will need to add in comments any additional residence history until you have completed two years.	Rental history is an excellent place to refer to when you have an application that requires an exception. A common compensating factor is 'at current residence more than 5 years'.
Income/Debt Information	Debt load will be visible on the Credit Report but it is important to ask a client this information. There may be new debt that is not yet showing on the report but may crop up later in the process.	You will want to determine if the applicant's are able to afford the housing you have available and if there are any programs that they may qualify for to aid in rental housing payments.

Explanation of credit situation?	This is the opportunity for notes. Your clients will usually explain any information that is present on their credit report.	Gathering this information now allows you to pre-plan the application package, request any additional documentation that you may need and is an excellent reference if problems appear later in the leasing process.
Outcome	You will want to note what happened with the query. Some inquiries will be filed for follow-up some will go to the lease negotiation process. This information allows you to track your numbers in future months.	

Because property management is a service business, the most important "product" that you have is the professionalism, attentiveness, and responsiveness that you show the tenants and the property owner. In the Property Management business, much of your communication will be on the telephone.

Whether you are communicating with a client, prospect or others on the telephone or in person, the impression that you convey creates an image in the person's mind that may be the basis of your future relationship with that person. It is important that your conversations are controlled and concise. The following pages will assist you in effectively managing telephone contacts to ensure the conversation proceeds in the manner you require.

The pre-qualification questionnaire offers an excellent tool for structuring your first contact.

PM: Good morning/afternoon/evening, _____ Rentals this is <u>Your Name</u>, may I help you?

Caller: The caller will state the reason for there call and very likely explain their situation.

PM: Do you have a few minutes to answer a couple of questions?

Caller: Since they made the call to you, they will typically have a few minutes to spare while they determine if you have a program to fit their situation.

PM: Could you tell me how you were referred to us?

PM: What is your name?

PM: Will you be on lease alone or with someone else?

PM: What is your Date of Birth?

PM: What is your Social Security Number?

PM: May I run a credit report?
You are looking for a yes. None of the other information you acquire will aid you in any way if you cannot see what type of credit situation you are dealing with. In addition, the approval to run a credit report signifies a commitment on the part of the caller to your rental property.

PM: Where are you employed?

PM: How long have you been there?
If they have been at their current employment less than two years, you will need to acquire two full years' employment history before completing the application.

PM: What is your position?

PM: Ask for the same information for the co-borrower.

PM: What is your current address?

PM: How long have you lived there?

PM: Do you rent or own the home?

PM: Who is your property owner or mortgage holder?
If the property owner or lender is a company there is no need for further documentation, it will be provided on the credit report. However, if their landlord/mortgage holder is an individual, more documentation will be required to prove a mortgage/rental history.

PM: Do you know what type of apartment you are looking for?

PM: Do you know the amount you are looking to spend?
This question allows you to determine from the start if their spending expectations are set too low for some of your rental units and place them accordingly.

PM: What is your monthly income?

You will often need to do the math yourself.

PM: Do you have income from any other source like alimony, child support etc?

PM: Obtain the same information for the co-borrower.

PM: What is your monthly rent/mortgage payment?

PM: What is your car payment?

PM: Do you have a second car?

PM: Do you have any credit cards or personal loans? What are the monthly payments?

Throughout the questionnaire, the caller will be giving you information that you will want to note in the explanation of credit situation section. This aids you in determining the special circumstances surrounding this application package.

Upon completion of the questionnaire, you will want to assure the caller that they are your clients.

You will need to set an appointment to meet face-to-face to verify their information and discuss their leasing options. A sample of how to do this smoothly is as follows:

PM: Ok, I plan to look over your information tonight to see what apartments I can offer you. Are you available <u>date not more than two days away</u>?

Caller: Answers positive or negative

PM: Set up an appointment.

PM: Ok then, I will see you on <u>date</u> at <u>time</u> if there are any problems, please give me a call.

Upon completion of the questionnaire, you will be able to pre-qualify a potential tenant. After you obtain the prospective tenant's permission, your next step is to pull a credit report and review it to determine initial rental levels and possible units that might suit their credit, income, and needs.

Today you make most of your contacts with people over the telephone. If you review your list of tasks and the times per day, you complete each task, the telephone contacts will no doubt outnumber any other task on the list.

One capability you must obtain is the ability to maintain control of conversations. The ability to maintain control of each conversation provides many vital benefits.

- You communicate more effectively.

- You will obtain and relay the required information in a more time efficient manner.

- You will be able to check the telephone task off your list and move on to the next important task.

In today's high pressure, fast-paced business world time is a commodity we cannot afford to waste. Many of us spend hours a week on one of the biggest time consumers in an average workday. We make telephone calls that aimlessly wander from subject to subject with no apparent core purpose. This wandering conversation loses valuable time and causes many people to fall behind their planned schedule. By learning conversational control techniques, you can minimize the likelihood of this happening in your workday.

Managing Outgoing Calls

When you are preparing to make a telephone call, you will have specific goals in place. You can achieve your goals if you plan the conversation and follow four simple steps.

- Clearly and concisely, control the call.

- Convey the information necessary.

- Obtain the necessary information.

- End the call.

You must do all of these tasks with professionalism and the customer service oriented personality that makes it a pleasure to receive a call from you.   Before placing any call, you should ask yourself some important questions about the call.

1. Why am I making this call?

2. What information do I need to obtain from this call?

3. What information must I convey with this call?

4. Is the information I must convey vital enough that I must speak directly with the person?

5. Can I include the necessary information in a message?

This may look like an inefficient list of questions to take time answering before each call but it is not. The time saved by minimizing aimless conversation and return calls will have a dramatic impact on the overall time you have invested in telephone calls each day.

You will soon be in the habit of knowing these answers before you make any call.

Until you have retrained, your habits to incorporate this list of questions into each telephone call efficiently and without conscious thought you will want to keep this list of questions taped under your telephone area. Before placing any call, you should generate a list of answers to each question for each contact on your task list or in the contact journal entries.

This reminder system will soon become an unnecessary function for you, but initially it will be vital in training your mind and habits to control conversational flow.

Managing Incoming Calls

The previous pages explained to you how to prepare for and control the flow of outgoing calls. Your workday will also contain a number of incoming calls that equal or even exceed your outgoing calls. You must become proficient at controlling the flow of incoming calls just as you would an outgoing call.

The pre-qualification questionnaire and the scripting included in this chapter will assist you in managing incoming calls from a prospective tenant. The effective management of other types of calls will assist you in managing your time, ensuring completeness in your communication and presenting a professional persona.

The people that you talk with during an incoming call have probably not completed a course like this one. They may not have the training or skills to conduct an efficient telephone call and to maximize both their time and yours. You must take control of incoming calls.

Earlier we suggested you place the list of conversational control questions right in front of your telephone. You can convert those same outgoing control questions to your incoming call control processes. You must train yourself to greet your incoming caller and then guide the conversation along the course that you know is the most time effective method.

Conversational Control Questions

1. What is the purpose of this call?

2. What information do I need to obtain during this call?

3. What information do I need to obtain or convey during this call?

Allowing your incoming calls to wander until the caller reaches the point of their call is not a time efficient activity. You will often end the call without obtaining or conveying the essential information that stimulated the contact to place the call in the first place. Aimless conversational flow often causes both parties to forget the points of discussion.

Incoming Call control Process

1. Access the caller's records in your client management program during the greeting portion of the call.

If you do not have a computerized database management system, you should have a paper file system in place that will accomplish the same purpose.

2. Skim the last two or three entries to refocus the vital facts and business of that contact to the front of your thoughts.

    This access will provide you with clues as to the callers needs with the telephone call.

    Example: If your last contact with the client was to schedule an appointment for a future date, the contact will likely be calling to confirm the appointment.

    Example: If your last contact with the client was to request information, the client is likely calling to confirm you received the requested documentation.

    Having clues that point you toward the purpose of the call allows you to address each question on your control question list.

3. Ask yourself the essential questions learned during incoming call-control training.

    Why am I receiving this call?

    What information do I need to obtain from this call?

    What information must I convey with this call?

4. Control the flow of the conversation, leading the caller to complete the call in an efficient, time effective manner.

5. Make notes in the caller's journal entry database during the call to ensure proper documentation.

You should note the answers to each question listed above so that you can control the course of the next contact in an efficient manner.

6. Learn the techniques to smoothly end a call and use them.

How Do Others Hear You?

While addressing telephone skills there are a few simple actions that you can take to make your messages and calls more pleasing to the other party allowing you to project a professional and positive persona to each contact. The bulk of your daily contacts will be via the telephone. When speaking on the telephone, whether in person or through voice mail, you always want to be aware of the impression you are making on the other party. You can take some simple steps to ensure that you convey your professionalism and enthusiasm.

1. Plan your calls.

   Following the guidelines outlined in this chapter will allow you to plan each call before you begin dialing. Whether you speak with the person you are calling or reach their voice mail, forethought and planning allow you to speak effectively and concisely. Speaking effectively and concisely projects an impression that you are a truly efficient professional.

2. Take a deep breath.

   Before you begin speaking or leaving a message, take a deep breath so that your message contains limited interruptions and flows smoothly. Taking a deep breath also strengthens your voice giving your message more depth and power.

3. Smile before you speak.

   A smile on your face will transmit to your voice. A smile in your voice projects a positive attitude. This will cause the person you are calling to view you, your message and the requests you are making in your message in a more positive frame of mind.

4. Speak slowly, clearly and concisely.

   Exceptional diction is an essential element in leaving effective messages. The person you are calling should be able to understand each word of your message the first time that they listen. Speaking clearly and concisely makes the task of voice mail transcription easier for your contact and shows a professional attitude.

5. Repeat the focus points of your call in all messages.

   Repeating vital information allows the other to obtain the necessary information in one playing of the voice mail rather than requiring another playing. This shows a respect for the time of your contact.

6. Use proper telephone etiquette like greetings and closings.

Goal Setting

In order to be successful you must set goals! Goals should be SMART.

S   Specific

M   Measurable

A   Agreed upon (with your manager)

R   Realistic

T   Time bound or time phased

Production goals should be very specific

"To obtain 1 application per hour today."

Or

"To obtain 1.5 appointments per hour today."

Your average "show ratio" might be another goal. A show ratio is the number of appointments you set with prospective tenants that they actually keep.

"My show ration will be 70% or higher for appointments."

When you are ready to start receiving or making calls, the first thing you should do is write out your goal for this calling session on a blank sheet of paper. Keep the paper in a prominent location throughout the telephone session.

Have fun with the people that you call and create a positive atmosphere.

You must be and actor or actress, remember you are selling not telling.

You should be giving a performance, not a speech.

Attitude is 98% of your job!

Smile!

Follow the presentation

Smile!

Be enthusiastic

Smile!

Have fun

Smile!

Make many calls

Smile!

Put mirror by your phone

Smile!

Whenever you are speaking with a potential tenant or property owner, even when they have called you, there will be objections to your presentation and products.

Handling Objections

Use the following rebuttal procedure:

1. LISTEN to determine whether the objection is a red flag, caution, or a green flag

2. Offer reassurance to any objection and follow the rebuttal tips included in this section.

3. RETURN to the presentation. Your conversational control study has taught you to maintain control of the flow. You should always return immediately to the focus of your call.

Setting Appointments

When it comes to setting appointments, there are three essential items to remember:

1. Show confidence

2. Be assertive

3. Set the appointment - <u>DON'T ASK</u>.

No matter the marketing efforts, there are certain Keys to Success that you will want to remember:

- Make a lot of calls

- Show enthusiasm

- Follow the presentation

- Attitude is 98% of your success

Telephone Calls – The Introduction

How to Present the Introduction

Show enthusiasm!

Have you ever listened to a presentation in amazement or wondered what all the fuss was about?

They are selling enthusiasm.

You must show this type of enthusiasm to your property owner or prospective tenants.

Rule # 1 Maintain excitement

You cannot expect your customer to be excited about your call if you are not!

Fluctuate your voice level and emphasize key words and phrases.

Avoid speaking too softly or using a monotone.

Be careful not to pause or breathe immediately after emphasized words.

Emphasizing the key words helps you in two ways:

1.   It slows you down and makes you more conversational.

2.   The words you emphasize are those most likely to stick in the prospect mind.

Talk with the prospect, not at them.

Rule # 2 Use conversation control techniques

Many customers make and receive so many calls these days that they immediately try to find a reason not to listen to your presentation, even though this call could solve many of their residence problems.

This type of objection is not specific to your product.

Many customers also have preconceived notions of why they have called you.

They think that they are rent shopping or they think that they want to know a particular piece of information about your units.

What each caller actually wants is housing. Keep this in mind.

A caller who wants to ask a quick question and end the call is really waiting for you to take control of the conversation and tell them why they should use services for their property rental needs.

An incoming telephone call should follow the pre-qualification scripting.

What is a Qualified Lead?

DESIRE • INTEREST • COMMITMENT

A qualified lead will have a desire for your property. They must be planning to move or establish their home in a rental environment.

A qualified lead must have an interest in the housing that you have available. They must have an interest in saving money, securing better housing or setting up a household.

A qualified lead will show a commitment to the process. They must have a need to complete the process within a specific time and you must secure the commitment to act.

DESIRE • INTEREST • COMMITMENT

Every lead you obtain must have all these ingredients or it is <u>not</u> a lead. If you have only had one or two of these ingredients, then you will have a "no-show" or cancellation.

Objections

Every objection will fall into one of three categories:

Red   =   Stop

Yellow   =   Caution

Green   =   Go

A **Red Objection** is any objection or statement that disqualifies the renter.

> "I am not planning a move."

> "I am unemployed right not."

The only suitable action for a Red Objection is to terminate the phone call. Thank them for their time and stop there.

A **Yellow objection** is any objection that is not specific or is unclear.

> "I already have an apartment."

> "I do not think I would be interested."

When you hear a Yellow Objection, you should dig in! Ask specifically what they would not be interested in or ask a question that it is almost impossible to say NO to.

"You mean that you would not be interested in a chance to move to a complex that offers ...?"

A **Green Objection** is any objection that denotes future interest

"I don't have time to talk right now."

"My spouse handles our decisions and isn't home right now."

When you hear a Green Objection, you should use a rebuttal to move past the objection.

"I can certainly understand Mr. /Ms. __name__ that you would not want to make a decision without your wife/husband. That is why Your Company Name offers a free, no obligation pre-qualification ..."

Digging In

When someone objects before allowing you to tell him or her you have to offer, dig in to find out what his or her true objection is. It might be that they have just trained themselves to "turn off" at the sound of an unfamiliar voice on the other end of the phone.

Example: "I'm not interested."

What is this prospect saying? Well, to be honest, <u>you do not know</u> what they are really saying.

Guidelines for handling this type objection:

1. Never ask "why?"

2. Say, "Golly or Gee, what would make you say that?"

3. Act surprised that someone is not interested. Act as if this is the first person who ever told you this!

   Acting surprised breaks down their natural sales resistance and enables you to get to the root of their objection.

Rebuttal Structure

Listen

You have to listen closely to determine whether the objection is Red, Yellow, or Green. If it is red, end the call. If it is yellow, "dig in." If green, proceed to the next step.

Reassurance

You must let the prospect know that you heard their objection.

Example: "I can certainly understand that Mr. /Ms. _____.

Offer

You have to build or reconfirm a sense of urgency.

Create the feeling in the prospect mind that by listening to you they are gaining something or that by not listening they stand to lose out. You can do this by stressing that they could be living better right now!

Reassurance

Make the prospect feel that the decision is up to them.

You should say something to the effect of "You be your own judge." Or "Decide for yourself."

Return_____

You must get immediately back to the presentation without a pause.

You must maintain control.

Listen

Reassure

Offer (the actual rebuttal)

Reassure

Back to the presentation

Building Rapport

Listen

Two ears, one mouth for a reason! When selling by phone it is even more important to be a good listener.

Listen for statements involving their family, their work, or recreational activities.

3rd Parties

Use scenarios with your own relatives or friends involved

Example: Yes, my dad used to do that...

Example: You know I had an old college buddy that used to live in that area...

Flattery

Used sparingly, flattery can be very effective at keeping a prospect interested.

You must come across as sincere or the effect could be negative!

Example: A retired person tells you they are retired.

No, Mr. /Ms. _____, you do not sound old enough to be retired. You must have retired early!

Example: A female tells you that she is unemployed or is a homemaker.

Well, you have the toughest kind of full-time job! My grandmother used to tell me she worked 36 hours a day 8 days a week....

Conclusion

These are only a few examples of how you can build rapport. The only limit is your imagination and enthusiasm!

Problems to Avoid in Rapport Building

Do not overuse rapport. You will lose focus of your objective if you get too close to the prospect.

Do not be too patronizing with your comments.

Do not be afraid or too timid to ask questions (it will show through.)

Do not cut someone off in the middle of a sentence.

Do not lose control of the call!

SALES MEETINGS & SHOWINGS 5

It is important that you gain the ability to handle all tenant interviews and unit showings with competency and control.

You are the professional and must learn to control the flow of face-to-face meetings in much the same manner that you control the flow of telephone conversations. You should be able to lead the interview in the correct direction to secure an application.

You should have a schedule of tenant appointments based on your marketing but should be prepared to handle walk in prospects at any time throughout your business days. Walk in prospects are common in the property management field. A walk in prospect will have already pre-screened your units and determined that the housing that you have available is likely to suit their needs.

You should always great the prospect immediately after they enter the leasing office. If you are in the middle of the task, assure the prospect that you will be with them in a moment and then complete your present task as quickly as possible.

By greeting the prospect immediately, you are in effect creating a welcoming atmosphere that will aid the prospect in determining that this is a building or complex community in which they would like to live. Your first personal contact with each prospect will set the tone in that potential tenant's mind for the entire community.

Walk in prospects that you are unable to aid immediately due to a scheduled prospect or another matter should be given the prospect pre-qualification form for completion. This serves to occupy the prospect until you are able to meet with them and to provide the information that you will need to begin qualifying that prospect and planning possible rental units for them to view.

You will want to focus your entire attention on the prospect as soon as possible.

This does not mean rushing your current appointment, it simply means that each prospect is as important as the other is and both should be treated with the respectful, customer service oriented manner you have striven to develop. Always remember, any prospect that is in your office has a higher likelihood of becoming a tenant than a phone prospect or a marketing contact.

You should develop a process for handling unexpected walk in leads. A walk in process enables you to keep the prospect occupied while you transition from your current task. This plan will need to remain flexible, as each prospect will have different needs and desires. You should have the general plan laid out that you will customize to the prospect pre-qualification when you review the prospect form.

You should set aside time in each sales & showing meeting to review and confirm the information included on the pre-qualification form. This review will enable you to isolate any issues that may exist while helping to formulate the sales strategy you will use with that particular lead. You will want to use the pre-qualification information to decide what features or even what particular unit you will show the lead.

One of the first steps a leasing consultant will take with most prospective tenants is to show them a rental unit that might be of interest to them. If you have multiple units available, you should consider the needs of the potential tenant before selecting one to show.

Example: An individual tenant might prefer a second floor unit with higher security.

A tenant who has less mobility might prefer a first floor unit that offers easier access.

A tenant who works nights might prefer an upstairs unit while less foot noise from the neighbors.

A family grouping might prefer a unit that is closer to a pool or the parking area.

Think about your tenant's particular situation before choosing the specific unit that you will show or the complex features you will emphasize during the sales meeting and showing.

When you show a unit, always allow the prospect to enter the apartment first giving them a sense of "home" and allowing you to watch where they go and customize your sales pitch around areas that may be of interest to them.

In other words, you will want to sell the kitchen to the cook, sell the family or living room to the party planner, and sell the size of the bedrooms to a tenant with a larger family.

Regardless of what features of your complex are most interesting to your prospective tenant, knowing your units allows you to point out key features of interest that may not be immediately evident.

The following pages will assist you in planning your sales presentations. Customize the material to suit your personal sales style and the type of units you have available for rent.

Planning the Sales Presentation

It is important to have an overview of the sales call before meeting with a prospect. This overview is an outline of what you wish to accomplish during the presentation. You should take this checklist with you on each showing to ensure that you to stay on the program and to review your performance immediately following the presentation.

Reviewing your performance allows you to make constant improvement to your presentations.

GOAL	COMMENTS
Create rapport with the prospect.	
Clarify the home space needs of the prospect.	
Customize a general benefit statement around the needs of the prospect.	
Make a transition statement that clarifies any points that you are not sure about and allows you to flow smoothly into your presentation.	
"To help you find the best home to suit your needs, I need to clarify... Explain how you, your complex, and your units meet the specific needs of the prospect.	
Give the prospect a reinforcing summary of the features, benefits, and amenities that you know were of interest to them during the pre-qualification and showing.	
Discuss unit and pricing options with a focus on solving problems like obtaining more space or reducing maintenance rather than on the	

cost of the unit.

Ask the tenant if they would like to commit to an application. If you do not ask, you will lose potential tenants.

Showing Basics

Each day when you arrive at the complex, you will want to be sure both you and the complex present the most appealing image possible. The previous pages offer a variety of tips to assist you in presenting yourself. The appearance of the rental unit, building or complex is as important to the final sale as what you say, how you say it or any other action.

Before you show a unit, building or complex:

Pick up garbage around the building.

Air out the rooms

Do minor cleaning.

Before you choose a unit to show:

Greet the prospective tenant warmly.

Probe for information

Ask who, what, why, where, when questions.

Determine how the prospect heard about your unit.

Referral? Advertisement? Flier or Brochure?

Let the prospect do most of the talking.

Remember two-ears/one-mouth.

Based on their conversation, tell the prospect the benefits and features of your units that will be most interesting to them.

Show the Correct Apartment:

Use the information provided by the prospect to select the unit that will be of the most interest to them, not the unit you have the most interest in renting.

Allow the prospective tenant to enter the apartment first, to determine what areas will be most interesting to them.

Point out those items that address their concerns- security, quiet tenants, cleanliness, near to transportation, etc.

Sell the prospective tenant on the benefits and features of the apartment based on the interest elements discovered during your pre-qualification interview and general discussions with the prospect.

Show the prospective tenants the prominent features of each room and the building because a feature that you have not related directly to that prospect may be the one that sells them on the unit.

If there is more than one tenant, give them the privacy that they need to discuss the unit and make a decision by wandering into another room.

Close the prospective tenant:

Provide each prospective tenant with the opportunity to complete the application.

Selling Against the Competition

Before you can begin planning your marketing or sales presentation, you must assess the competition and what they have to offer compared to what you have to offer prospective tenants. The competition in rental property management is any other vacancy available in your area. Gaining an application from a well-qualified tenant is only useful if the tenant you choose as the best quality applicant is as interested in renting the unit that you have to offer, as you are interested in renting to them.

One method of ensuring that your units are the most desirable to the tenants you select is to compare your unit offerings, costs, sales techniques and special features against those offered by the competition. You should conduct a thorough investigation into the offerings of your competition. The answers that you discover during your investigation will direct you in creating a marketing plan that maximizes the features you have available while minimizing the items that might not be at the same level as those offered by the competition.

Who is the Competition?

Individual Building?

Complex?

What target market will the competition seek as applications?

Is the target market of this competitor the same as my target market?

What unit would the competition offer a prospect?

What negatives does that unit carry?

Do I have a unit that offers equal benefits and features to the one my competition will offer a prospect?

What payment would the competitions unit require?

Can I beat the price of the competing units?

Can I offer a better feature, service, or price than the competing property?

After investigating the competition, you should take any action available to you that helps to meet or exceed the features, benefits, or amenities that the competition will offer to a prospective tenant. You should also create a presentation that matches your unit's features, benefits and amenities to the needs of prospective tenants while minimizing any item that might not be equal to or surpass the offerings of the competition.

Prospect Summary

Date: _____ Applicant Name: _____

Time: _____ Purpose: _____

Outcome: _____

_____

Action Plan: _____

_____

Date: _____ Applicant Name: _____

Time: _____ Purpose: _____

Outcome: _____

_____

Action Plan: _____

_____

Date: _____ Applicant Name: _____

Time: _____ Purpose: _____

Outcome: _____

_____

Action Plan: _____

_____

Sample Prospect Summary

6

UNDERSTANDING THE RENTAL APPLICATION

Once you have impressed your prospective clients with your customer service skills and the value of the rental units that you have available, it is time to complete a rental lease application.

The purpose of this application is to obtain all of the information required to assess the potential tenant's credit worthiness and ability to rent from your firm or within your rental property. If the potential tenant meets the income and credit guidelines set forth by the property owner or management firm, you will use the rental application information to assist them in completing a rental lease agreement.

Rental applications come in many forms. We have included two sample applications for you to review. These applications contain all of the basic components and information that will be required to assess the potential tenant's worthiness as an applicant. Worthiness is based upon the probability of a tenant paying their lease obligations as agreed. This worthiness is based upon items within the applications profile such as

Employment history

Previous rental history

Income

Credit history

Debt load

The worthiness determination should be made based only on factual information contained within the file. The assessment should be the same for all potential tenants. You should never use qualifiers like race, religion, familial status, handicap status or other factors that could be considered discriminatory to assess a potential tenant worthiness.

The application examples include the basic information necessary for the screening of a prospective tenant. You should request a copy of the application used by your particular property owner or management firm or retain the services of a real estate professional in the composition of a residential rental application that will best meet your needs.

The following forms are modified from the publicly published forms released for use in real estate transactions from HUD and other applicable agencies. The forms are for example purposes only.

Residential Rental Application

Please complete the following application in its entirety.
All information obtained in the application will remain confidential.
Co-applicants who are not related must complete separate application forms.

Date: _____   Community: _____ Special Provisions: _____

Apt. #: _____   Monthly Rental: _____

Move-In: _____   Lease Term: _____ Leasing Consultant: _____

APPLICANT

Name: _____   DOB: _____

DL#: _____ State: _____   SSN: _____

Employer: _____   Phone: _____

Address: _____   Income: _____

Position: _____   # Yrs: _____

Supervisor: _____   Phone: _____

Previous Employer: _____   # Yrs: _____

Present Address: _____

How Long?_____ Reason for Leaving: _____

Owner or Agent Name:_____ Phone:_____

Rental Payment:_____ Were you ever late making a payment? _____

If yes, explain: _____

_____

CO-APPLICANT

Name: _____ DOB: _____

DL#: _____ State: _____ SSN: _____

Employer: _____ Phone:_____

Address:_____ Income:_____

Position:_____ # Yrs: _____

Supervisor:_____ Phone:_____

Previous Employer:_____ # Yrs: _____

Present Address:_____

How Long?_____ Reason for Leaving: _____

Owner or Agent Name:_____ Phone:_____

Rental Payment:_____ Were you ever late making a payment? _____

It yes, explain: _____

_____

Other Occupants: _____ Relationship:_____

Other Occupants: _____ Relationship:_____

Other Occupants: _____ Relationship:_____

Pets(type/weight):_____

Pets (type/weight):_____

Credit Information:

Creditor	Monthly Payment	Account Number
_____	_____	_____
_____	_____	_____
_____	_____	_____

Bank Checking Account   Bank Savings Account

_____   _____

Emergency Contact

Name: _____   Relationship: _____

Address: _____   Phone: _____

I hereby apply to lease the aforementioned premises for the term set forth. I warrant that all statements set forth are true and correct.

I hereby deposit $_____ as earnest money to be refunded to me if this application is not accepted. Upon acceptance, this deposit shall be applied toward security deposit and/or the first months rent for the described property. I hereby waive any claim for damages due to non-acceptance. Owner or agent may reject my application without stating any reason for doing so.

I understand that if I decide that I do not wish to sign a lease for the apartment, I must notify the leasing agent or office within 48 hours of signing below. I understand that if I fail to do so I will forfeit my earnest money deposit.

I recognize that as part of the procedure for processing my application an investigative consumer credit report may be prepared and verified through other channels. I authorize these sources to release such information, as the leasing company deems necessary. The lease may be cancelled without further notice if any of the information contained herein proves inaccurate.

Signature of Applicant: _____   Date: _____

Signature of Co-Applicant: _____   Date: _____

Signature of Agent: _____   Date: _____

Earnest Money Deposit: $_____

RENTAL APPLICATION
Equal Housing Opportunity

The undersigned hereby makes an application to rent unit #_____
located at: _____.
Anticipated move date of _____at a monthly rent of
$_____ and security deposit of $_____.

PLEASE TELL US ABOUT YOURSELF

Full Name_____ Home Phone _____

Date of Birth_____ Social Security _____

Email Address:_____(optional) Other Phone _____

Co-Applicant Name_____ Other Phone _____

Date of Birth_____ Social Security _____

Dependents Date of Birth_____

List All Pets_____

PLEASE GIVE RESIDENTIAL HISTORY (LAST 3 YEARS)

Current Address_____

Apt#_____ City_____ State_____ Zip_____

Month/Year Moved In_____ Rent $_____

Reasons for Leaving _____

Owner/Agent_____ Phone _____

Previous Address (last 3 years)_____Rent $_____

Owner/Agent_____ Phone _____

PLEASE DESCRIBE YOUR CREDIT HISTORY

Have you declared bankruptcy in the past seven (7) years? Yes_____ No_____

Have you ever been evicted from a rental residence? Yes_____ No_____

Have you had two or more late rental payments in the past year? Yes_____ No_____

Have you ever willfully or intentionally refused to pay rent when due? Yes_____ No_____

PLEASE PROVIDE YOUR EMPLOYMENT INFORMATION

Your Status: ____Full Time ____Part Time ____Student ____Unemployed

Employer_____

Dates employed_____ Employed as_____

Supervisor Name_____ Phone _____

Salary $_____per_____.

(If employed by above less than 12 months, give name & phone of previous employer or

_____

If you have other sources of income that you would like us to consider, please list income, source, and person (banker, employer, etc.) who we may contact for confirmation. You do not have to reveal alimony, child support, or spouse's annual income unless you want us to consider it in this application.

Amount $_____
Source/Contact Name_____

PLEASE LIST YOUR REFERENCES
Banking Accounts:

Name_____ Type of Account_____ Account #_____

Name_____ Type of Account_____ Account #_____

Personal Reference or Emergency Contact:

Name _____

Address_____

Phone _____   Relationship_____

Driver's License:

Driver's License Number_____ State_____

Vehicle Information:

Make / Model _____Year _____License Plate _____

ADDITIONAL INFORMATION:

Please give any additional information that might help owner / management evaluate this application?

_____

_____

_____

_____

Where may we reach you to discuss this application?

Day Phone _____   Night Phone _____

I hereby apply to lease the above described premises for the term and upon the set conditions above set forth and agree that the rental is to be payable the first day of each month in advance.

I warrant that all statements above set forth are true; however, should any statement made above be found to be a misrepresentation or not a true statement of facts, all of the deposit will be retained to offset the agent's cost, time, and effort in processing my application.

I hereby deposit $_____ as earnest money to be refunded to me if this application is not accepted in 3 business banking days. Upon acceptance, this deposit shall be retained as part of the security deposit. When so approved and accepted, I agree to execute a lease for _____ months before possession is given and to pay the balance of the security deposit before the move in date.

If the application is not approved or accepted by the owner or agent, the deposit will be refunded, the application hereby waiving any claim for damages by reason off non-acceptance which the owner or agent may reject.

I recognize that as a part of your procedure for processing my application, and investigative consumer report may be prepared whereby information is obtained through personal interviews with others with whom I may be acquainted. This inquiry includes information as to my character, general reputation, personal characteristics and mode of living.

The above information, to the best of my knowledge, is true and correct.

AUTHORIZATION
Release of Information

I agree to permit an investigation of my credit, tenant history, banking and employment for the purposes of renting an apartment with this owner/manager.

_____
Name (please print)

_____   _____
Signature   Date

COMPLIANCE – FAIR HOUSING

7

Screening prospective tenants is an important component of the property manager's job. The type of tenants that you secure is critical to your success and to the profitability of the investment property.

You must secure tenants who are financially responsible and able to afford the cost of your rental. The tenants you secure must also be the type of people that will treat the unit and surrounding areas in a careful and respectful manner.

The goal of any property owner or management firm is to secure long-term tenants who pay in a timely manner and do not cause undue damage to the building.

The first and perhaps most vital component of tenant screening is compliance with all of the laws and regulations regarding housing.

Whenever you are interviewing a prospective tenant or accepting a residential lease application, there are certain laws to which you must adhere.

The Federal Civil Rights act of 1866 states that all citizens of the United States shall have "the same rights as enjoyed by white citizens to inherit, purchase, lease, sell, hold, and covey real and personal property". This act prohibits discrimination based on race and color. There are no exemptions to this act.

The US Supreme Court upheld this law in 1968 by stating that this law prohibits all racial discrimination both public and private. The Civil Rights Act is referred to in the Fair Housing Law and identifies the classes that are protected. It is prohibited to discriminate against any individual based on race, religion, color, sex, national origin or familial status.

A building may be excluded from these regulations if the building is designated by HUD as designed specifically to assist elderly persons and is intended to be occupied solely by persons 62 years of age or older.

The Federal Civil Rights Act of 1968 also protects people with handicapped status. The act does not provide protection for those individuals with an addiction to illegal controlled substances. Under the Act, a handicapped person must be given the right to make reasonable modifications to the property at the handicapped person's expense. These modifications must be related to the individual's ability to obtain full enjoyment of the property.

Federal Fair Housing Law has mandated the following actions as against Federal Regulations.

- Blockbusting for profit or persuading owners to sell or rent housing by telling them those minority groups are moving into the neighborhood.

- Denying or making different terms or conditions for the obtainment of housing to certain individuals

- Denying anyone the use of a real estate service offered to the public.

Prohibitions contained in the Fair Housing Law apply to the following types of Housing:

- Single-Family housing owned by private individuals when a broker or other person in business is selling or renting the dwelling.

- Single-Family housing owned by a private individual who owns more than three such houses or who, in any two-year period, sells more than one property in which the individual was not the most recent resident

- Multifamily dwellings of five or more units

- Multifamily dwellings containing four or fewer units, if the owner does not reside in one of the units

These provisions make it illegal to coerce, intimidate, threaten or interfere with a person's ability to buy, rent or sell housing.

As a professional Property Manager, you may not refuse to deal or negotiate with any person, discriminate in the terms offered for renting housing by any individual, or use discriminatory language in any advertising.

You can help to ensure that you comply with the Federal Laws governing rental housing by relying only on the factual information contained within the lease application and related credit report when screening potential tenants for your managed property.

QUALIFYING TENANTS

8

The property owner will have specific requirements for the assessment of tenant suitability. One of these requirements will often pertain to the credit reports of the perspective tenant. The following pages will provide an overview of credit reports. It is important you gain an understanding of how to read a credit report and assess an individual's credit worthiness based on the information contained within the report. Credit reports are one of the most essential elements in determining a potential tenant's suitability.

Every action that a consumer takes affects their credit report. These actions can have a negative or a positive effect.

Credit reports are an overview of a person's history of spending and payment habits. Almost everything that a person does financially is collected, reported, and stored in the credit profile. The primary concern of during the rental screening process is any action that had a negative or derogatory impact on a potential tenant's credit history.

Debt is the term describing any situation where money is owed and is repaid under a repayment agreement.

Debt Load is the amount of debt an individual is carrying or the amount that the individual owes to another.

Debt load may include many items. The most common being:

Credit Card Debt
Department Store Debt
Charge Accounts

Auto Loans
Student Loans
Housing Costs

The ability to afford the rental payment required for the units that you have available is dependant on how much debt a prospective tenant currently carries compared to their available income.

You will be concerned with the debt-to-income ratio of the tenant.

Debt-to-Income Ratio's are the amount of open debt a tenant carries weighed against the tenant's monthly income. The higher the DTI the greater the potential risk that the tenant will fail to complete the lease.

The credit report will provide a relatively accurate view of the tenant's current debt load. You must document the tenant's income in order to have the information necessary to calculate the debt-to-income ratio.

Late payments are any payments that have been paid more than 30-days past the due date. Late payments can be a severe blemish on the credit report. You will need to rate late payments based on how late the payment was made by the potential tenant. You will also need to assess the frequency with which the late payments occurred. Most property owners will have limits on the number of late payments that are acceptable over the previous 12-24 month period. A late payment will appear on the credit report for two years, though credit bureaus may keep them in the credit file for up to seven years.

Bankruptcy actions can remain on the credit report for as long as 10 years. A bankruptcy is a significant factor that must be considered when ranking a potential tenant. Some property owner's will accept a tenant as soon as the bankruptcy has been discharged while others will require that the tenant establish a new credit history before allowing them to enter into a lease agreement.

Collection accounts are accounts that a borrower has failed to pay as agreed and that the creditor is attempting to collect.

These accounts are frequently turned over to a collection department within the structure of the original creditor, a collection agency, or another service in the attempt to collect the payments owed. The collection account may appear on the credit report multiple times since the initial creditor and the collection agencies may all report these accounts to the bureaus.

If a collection account appears on the report more than one time, you should remit a credit supplement request to the credit bureau asking that these duplicate entries be condensed to reflect that the entries all refer to one account. This may assist in raising the credit score of the potential tenant.

If your tenant has paid any collection account in full, have them obtain a letter from the creditor stating that the debt has been satisfied and that no further action on their part is necessary.

Property owners will handle collection accounts in different ways. Some will allow a certain dollar amount of collections to remain open while others will require all of the collection accounts be paid in full before the tenant is eligible for a lease. Some property owners will handle medical collection accounts differently than other accounts.

You will want to consider the type and amount of collections that the potential tenant has open when you review the credit report.

Medical collections are accounts owed to medical service providers that the potential tenant has failed to pay. Medical collection accounts are often treated differently than other collection accounts. You will need to consider the type of collection accounts in the profile and review the property owner's guidelines to determine how to handle each type of account.

Credit inquiries are accesses to an individual's credit profile. These inquiries are visible on the credit report. A series of inquiries could also indicate that new credit obligations are present but not visible on the report. If the potential tenant has new debt that is not yet showing up on the report, you should discuss their ability to pay the rent on the unit over the coming months.

Credit Bureau Scores are the scores generated based solely on the data contained within the credit report. A Fair Isaac Credit Bureau Score, is sometimes referred to as a FICO score. The FICO Score is calculated using a system of scorecards. Credit scoring has been around since the 1950's and Credit Bureau Scores became widely available in the 1980's. Credit Scores are now used extensively in such industries as rental housing, mortgage lending, auto lending, and bankcards. A Credit Bureau Score is a scientific way of assessing how likely a borrower is to pay back a loan.

The **Score Range** of the Fair Isaac Credit Bureau Score is approximately 450 to 850 points. Credit scores are available through three national repositories.

The scoring programs of these credit bureaus are called:

BEACON	at EQUIFAX (CBI)
EMPIRICA	at TRANS UNION
TRW/FAIR, ISAAC	at TRW

The credit score is calculated at the repository and is based on the data available with in the individual's credit report. A credit bureau score is not a measure of an individual's income, assets, or bank account. A credit bureau score is simply a rank ordering of an individual's likelihood to pay debts as agreed.

In developing the credit scorecards, Fair Isaac uses actual credit data from millions of consumers. They apply complex mathematical formulas and perform extensive research into credit patterns that enable them to forecast credit performance. Through this process, the repository identifies distinctive credit patterns. Each pattern corresponds to likelihood that a consumer will make his or her loan payments as agreed. This score is based on all of the credit-related data in the credit bureau report, not just negative data such as a missed payment or a bankruptcy.

The score will consider the amount of credit a borrower has available, the amount of credit the borrower is using compared to these limits, the types of credit a borrower has available, and the borrowers payment performance on their credit obligations among other factors.

Information used to develop the scorecard is gathered from every aspect of an individual's payment and spending history. These can include

Payment history
Public records
Collection items
Severity, recentness, and frequency of delinquencies
Outstanding debt
Number of balances recently reported
Average balance across all trade lines
Relationship between total balances and total credit limits on revolving trade lines
Credit History
Age of oldest trade line
Inquiries and new account openings
Number of inquiries in the last year
Number of new accounts opened in the last year
Amount of time since the most recent inquiry
Types of credit in use
Number of trade lines for each type pf credit
    Bankcard
    Travel and Entertainment cards
    Department Store cards
    Personal Finance Company references
    Installment Loans
    Other credit

Fair Isaac observes tens of thousands of credit report histories to determine which credit report items or combination of items are the most predictive of future risk. This data indicates the amount of weight each item should contribute to a credit decision.

THE FAIR ISAAC CREDIT BUREAU SCORES DO NOT USE RACE, COLOR, RELIGION, NATIONAL ORIGIN, SEX, MARITAL STATUS, OR AGE AS PREDICTIVE CHARACTERISTICS.

OCCUPATION AND LENGTH OF TIME IN PRESENT HOUSING ARE NOT USED IN THE SCORECARDS.

ANY INFORMATION THAT IS NOT PRESENT IN THE CREDIT FILE IS NOT USED IN CREATING A CREDIT BUREAU SCORECARD.

Understanding a score's impact

The credit report will contain one or multiple credit scores followed by a series of score factor reason codes. This numerical score is often termed a fair Isaac credit bureau score and it is a means of rank ordering potential borrowers based on the likelihood that they will pay their credit obligations as agreed.

A higher score indicates a better credit quality. If all other things in the profile were equal, an individual with a credit score of 642 is more likely to pay their debts as agreed than an individual with a score of 537.

The Fair Isaac Credit Bureau Score models at each credit repository are of similar design. The scores are scaled to indicate a similar level of risk across all three repositories. In other words, a score of 660 at one bureau will represent a similar level of risk as a score of 660 at another bureau.

The risk denoted by the credit score is defined as the number of accounts remaining in good standing compared to those accounts that contain derogatory data or that have gone into default.

Sample credit score ranges for new borrowers from a national sample

Score Range	Number of good loans for each delinquency (# of good to 1 bad)
Below 600	8 to 1
700 – 719	123 to 1
Above 800	1,292 to 1

Figure 7:1 Sample Score Range

Credit bureau scores will rank order individuals based on risk or the number of good loans to bad loans denoted by the score. This rank order is likely to fluctuate depending on changes in the economy, regional differences, changes in credit guidelines and other reasons.

A property owner who uses scores for rank order potential tenants is basing their guideline tiers of risk on historical data related to the files that they have processed in the past. The levels or approval tier that the property owner uses is likely to fluctuate over time due to changes in the economy.

Report Appearance

Credit reports can take multiple visual forms depending on the bureau that issued the report and the type of record being requested. Regardless of the initial visual variations, all credit reports contain the same basic elements. These include individual details and data, a summary of all of the credit inclusions, and a detailed breakdown of the individual's current and historical credit transactions. Each section of the report will contain details that will assist you in determining if the potential tenant will qualify for one of your rental units.

The upper portion of credit report will typically include identifying information including your name or company name as the individual, who requested the report.

Report type will usually be included in the header. Report type may be individual or joint.

Information relating to the individual within the credit bureau who pulled the report and the internal case ID # assigned to the report will be defined in the header of the report. This information will be important if you must request updates to the report or address a discrepancy in the report with the credit bureau.

MERGED INFILE CREDIT REPORT

Prepared For:	Property Address:	Prepared By:	Date Rec:
Attention:	Loan Type: Purpose of Loan: Report Type:	Computer ID: Lender Case #:	Date Comp: Date Revised:

APPLICANT

Name:		
SSN:	DOB:	
Marital Status:	Dependents:	
Home Phone:		
Present Address:		
Since:	Own / Rent	
Previous Address:		

CO-APPLICANT

Name:		
SSN:	DOB:	
Marital Status:	Dependents:	
Home Phone:		
Present Address:		
Since:	Own / Rent	
Previous Address:		

Date data will be included within the report. Date data can include the date the request was received by the credit bureau, the date the credit bureau completed the report, and the date of any revisions created by the credit bureau in relationship to the report.

Figure 7:2 Example - Credit Report Extract / Explanation

Borrower Information

The credit report will contain details relating to the individual or individuals to whom the credit report applies.

This portion includes specifics such as full name, social security number, and date of birth. Information relating to the individuals address and employment may be included in this segment of the report. It is important that you remember that information you have gained directly from the potential tenant may be more up-to-date than information contained within the credit report.

Variations in the address and employment are common within the report. You should note any discrepancy between the report and your file information and verify with the potential tenant to ensure that the report does not contain entries that relate to another individual with a similar name.

MERGED INFILE CREDIT REPORT			
Prepared For:	Property Address:	Prepared By:	Date Rec:
Attention:	Loan Type:	Computer ID:	Date Comp:
	Purpose of Loan:		
	Report Type:	Lender Case #:	Date Revised:

APPLICANT   CO-APPLICANT

Name:		Name:	
SSN:	DOB:	SSN:	DOB:
Marital Status:	Dependents:	Marital Status:	Dependents:
Home Phone:		Home Phone:	
		Present Address:	
Present Address:			
		Since:	Own / Rent
Since:	Own / Rent	Previous Address:	
Previous Address:			

Borrower and Co-Borrower identifying information is entered in this section.

You should verify that all details entered match the information included on the rental application.

Figure 7:3 Example - Credit Report Extract / Explanation

Credit Summary

The credit report will contain a segment that summarizes the details contained within the actual report. You should review this area to ensure that the inclusions do not contain information that will present a barrier to renting to the potential tenant. You may need to question the potential tenant more closely regarding these entries.

CREDIT SUMMARY

	PAYMENTS	BALANCE	LIMITS	TRADES	30+	60+	90+
REVOLVING	0	2061	2200	4	4	4	17
INSTALLMENT	1307	79365	90610	25	34	8	27
REAL ESTATE	378	35384	36600	1	2	0	0
OPEN/OTHER	991	1041	1041	5	0	0	0
TOTAL	2676	117851	129451	38	40	12	44

INQUIRIES   50   # PUBLIC RECORDS   0   # BANKRUPTCIES
0
WORST TRADE 9   OLDEST DATE 07/01/89   #
SATISFACTORIES   17

The summary will contain details identifying the types of credit that the potential tenant has available. You wish to ensure that the types and amount of credit available to the potential tenant is exported into the DTI Analysis Form.

If you are using a system that does not automatically export report data into the Analysis Forms, you will need to enter each credit account, payment, and status by hand.

Credit payment totals and current balances will appear within the credit summary portion of the report.

You will confirm the payment information when you review the report inclusions.

Then you will use this information to confirm the debt ratio information submitted by the potential tenant.

A summary data analysis of the details of the report will be included. This analysis will assist you in completing the scoring key. Much of the data you will use during credit scoring will be summarized with in this section. Before you export the data into the credit-scoring key, debt-to-income ratio form, or application, you must review the report with the potential tenant to ensure that all of the inclusions of the summary are correct and relate to active accounts.

Figure 7:4 Example - Credit Report Extract / Explanation

CREDIT SUMMARY

	PAYMENTS	BALANCE	LIMITS	TRADE	30+	60+	90+
REVOLVING	0	2061	2200	4	4	4	17
INSTALLMENT 1307	1307	79365	90610	25	34	8	27
REAL ESTATE	378	35384	36600	1	2	0	0
OPEN/OTHER	991	1041	1041	5	0	0	0
TOTAL	2676	117851	129451	38	40	12	44

INQUIRIES   50   # PUBLIC RECORDS   0   # BANKRUPTCIES   0
WORST TRADE 9   OLDEST DATE 07/01/89   # SATISFACTORIES   17

The number of inquiries into credit profile will be totaled and entered into the summary.

A detailed breakdown of the companies that made credit inquiries will be included at the end of the report.

The potential may be required to provide an explanation for any excessive inquiries.

Credit inquiries may indicate that the potential tenant has additional debt that is not yet showing on the credit report or may be related to the search for housing.

If the potential tenant is not aware of the recent inquiries, this may be an indication of fraud and the potential tenant should review all of the entries on their report in case they are a victim of identity theft.

Specifics regarding public records, bankruptcy, and the worst trade payment history that you will encounter in the report will be included within the credit summary.

You should note these entries to ensure that you locate the applicable data within the report relating to any bankruptcy, late payment, or public record detailed within the summary.

Each property owner will have specific requirements related to public records, bankruptcy actions, and poor credit history.

Figure 7:5 Example - Credit Report Extract

CREDIT SUMMARY

	PAYMENTS	BALANCE	LIMITS	TRADES	30+	60+	90+
REVOLVING	0	2061	2200	4	4	4	17
INSTALLMENT	1307	79365	90610	25	34	8	27
REAL ESTATE	378	35384	36600	1	2	0	0
OPEN/OTHER	991	1041	1041	5	0	0	0
TOTAL	2676	117851	129451	38	40	12	44

INQUIRIES   50   # PUBLIC RECORDS   0   # BANKRUPTCIES   0

WORST TRADE 9   OLDEST DATE 07/01/89   # SATISFACTORIES   17

The oldest date field indicates the date that the potential tenant fist obtained credit.

This inclusion allows you to ensure that an adequate credit history is available to the potential tenant. Many property owners will require the potential tenant has at least a two-year credit history with at least three open active trade lines. If your potential tenant does not have a sufficient credit history or quantity of accounts, you may need to take alternative actions to aid the tenant in creating a credit profile that meets the minimum requirements of the property owner guidelines.

It is important to address any issues early in the prequalification process. Proactively addressing issues early in the process helps to minimize stipulation requests, speeds the rental process, and facilitates positive relationships with tenant, the property owner, and affinity service providers. This positive relationship building activity helps to ensure that you gain the reputation as the property manager that can get the job done.

Figure 7:6 Example - Credit Report Extract

Score Factors

The name of the repository issuing the credit score included with the report will be included.

The property manager will designate which of the 3 credit repository scores is applicable for your potential tenant.

This designation is a result of regional variations regarding reported matters making one repository more complete than another does.

The code of the applicable agency will be entered to confirm the source of the score.

EFX = Equifax

8   BEACON SCORE   EFX01
            519
            SERIOUS DELINQUENCY AND DEROGATORY PUBLIC RECORD OR COLLECTION FILED
            AMOUNT OWED ON DELINQUENT ACCOUNTS
            PROPORTION OF BALANCES TO CREDIT LIMITS TOO HIGH ON REVOLVING ACCOUNTS
            LENGTH OF TIME ACCOUNTS HAVE BEEN ESTABLISHED

8   EMPIRICA SCORE   TRU01
            493
            SERIOUS DELINQUENCY, AND PUBLIC RECORD OR COLLECTION FILED
            LEVEL OF DELINQUENCY ON ACCOUNTS
            TIME SINCE DELINQUENCY IS TOO RECENT OR UNKNOWN
            PROPORTION OF REVOLVING BALANCES TO REVOLVING CREDIT LIMITS IS TOO HIGH

8   FAIR ISAAC SCORE   XPN01
            529
            SERIOUS DELINQUENCY AND PUBLIC RECORD OR COLLECTION FILED
            PROPORTION OF BALANCES TOO HIGH ON REVOLVING ACCOUNTS
            NUMBER OF ACCOUNTS DELINQUENT
            LENGTH OF TIME SINCE LEGAL ITEM FILED OR COLLECTION ITEM REPORTED

The factors that affect the score will be included on the report. This information is often referred to as score factor code.

Figure 7:7 Example - Credit Report Extract

Score Factors – Reason Codes

To understand why a credit report scored the way it did, you must review the reason codes given within each score. These reason codes provide the top reasons why a profile did not score higher. These codes only indicate the top reasons and other factors probably contribute to the overall score. You should review both the score and the reasons the score ranks where it does with your potential tenant.

To find the scores, you should locate a number or a letter followed by a brief description.

For example, a score of 540 may have the following factors

- 02 – Delinquency on accounts
- 01 – Amount owed on accounts is too high
- 09 – Too many accounts opened in the last 12 months
- 19 – Too few accounts currently paid as agreed

Score factors are less meaningful for higher scoring credit records as they merely point to the reasons why a very good credit report was not perfect.

Examples of adverse factors that may appear on the report as a consideration in the score computation are

- Current outstanding balances on accounts
- Delinquency report on accounts
- Accounts not paid as agreed
- Too few open accounts
- Too many open accounts
- Too many bank accounts with outstanding balances
- Too many finance company accounts
- Payment history too new to rate
- Number of inquiries within the last 12 months
- Number of accounts opened within the last 12 months
- Balance too high
- Length of credit history
- No recent account information

- Too few accounts rate as current
- Amount past due on accounts
- No adverse factors
- Recent derogatory public record or collection

This is not an all-inclusive listing. The items listed are examples of issues you may find in the score coding section of a report. You should review each report carefully to determine the factors specific to that credit profile.

Fraud Alert

The fraud alert field is becoming increasingly filled field within today's environment. Any data that indicates possible fraud activity will be included with in this section. The information will often become a warning entry because of some action taken by the individual but any entry other than "*available and clear*" should be reviewed and discussed with the potential tenant.

Basic information noted by the credit bureau as potential fraud will be flagged.

If the entry is not related to an action taken by the potential tenant, the tenant may be a victim of identity theft and all entries in the body of the report should be scrutinized to ensure that all of the accounts do belong to the potential tenant.

An example of a fraud alert entry would be the number of inquiries in the last 60 days.

Excessive inquiries may be a result of the housing shopping process. In this case, there is little cause for concern as the alert is related to an action taken by your potential tenant. However, excessive inquiries could indicate access to the credit profile by another party who is seeking to open fraudulent accounts in your potential tenant's name.

1	TRANS ALERT	TRU01
	# INQUIRIES IN LAST 60 DAYS: 04	
	RECORDED INQUIRIES ALTER	

| 1 | HAWK ALERT | TRU 01 |
| | HAWK AVAILABLE AND CLEAR | |

Details regarding any activity that may indicate fraud will be included.

AVAILABLE AND CLEAR   =   No information found

inquiries in the last 60 days =   potential credit gathering spree.

At times, this could indicate a stolen profile but more often, this insert is related to the search current loan search.

Figure 7:9 Example - Credit Report Extract / Explanation

Credit History Details

The main body of the report will contain details of each account contained within the credit history. You will wish to scrutinize each entry within this section to determine the status of the credit, gain an understanding of the payment and spending habits, and complete the credit history-scoring key.

CREDIT HISTORY

E C O A	CREDITOR ACCOUNT NO	DATE RPTD	DATE LAST ACT	DAT E OPN D	LIMIT / HIGHEST CREDIT	PRESENT STATUS		TERMS	PAY AMT	TYPE AND ACCT STATUS	HISTORICAL STATUS			
						BAL OWING	AMT PAST DUE				NO MOS HIIST REV	3 0	6 0	9 0
8	AFM-BLOOM #APRINTLO COLLECTIO N	02/99	04/94		425	425				OPN05				

The name of the creditor and the account number will be included within the report.

Account numbers are often shortened on the credit report and the full account number may not appear. You can obtain the full account number directly from your buyer if it is a necessary element of the funding process.

Figure 4:10 Example - Credit Report Extract / Explanation

CREDIT HISTORY

E C O A	CREDITOR ACCOUNT NO	DATE RPTD	DATE LAST ACT	DATE OPND	LIMIT / HIGHEST CREDIT	PRESENT STATUS		PAY AMT	TYPE AND ACCT STATUS	HISTORICAL STATUS			
						BAL OWING	AMT PAST DUE			NO MOS HIIST REV	3 0	6 0	9 0
8	AFM-BLOOM #APRINTLO COLLECTION	02/9 9	04/94		425	425			OPN05				

The date reported is the last reporting date for a particular account.

Not all creditors report on a monthly basis.

You may be required to bring the data pertaining to a specific account up to date to comply with property owner guidelines.

This up date status helps to ensure that no new derogatory data exists during the last months of the account,

The date last active information provides you with the details relating to the last date that the account was in use.

Some accounts will be old, closed accounts and will not affect the current transaction.

You should review the last active date before including an account within the credit history scoring.

The opening date of the account allows you to review the historical status with more accuracy.

Figure 7:11 Example - Credit Report Extract / Explanation

The present status details the current balances and any amounts currently due for each account.

You should scan this column to note any issues that may arise during the rental process.

Past due accounts may lead to a credit denial or change in the rental terms of credit offered to your potential tenant.

The terms field shows the original and the current agreement relating to the payments and terms of each account.

A revolving account or credit card will typically not provide you with the end date for the payments since these accounts will continue until one party cancels the relationship.

Installment notes will give you the payment terms agreed upon for the account.

Payment amount will show the minimum payment that is due for each account.

You will export these payment amounts into the DTI ratio calculation form.

If the account has no payment entered, it may be an inactive account or it may be a revolving account that does not have a balance.

Even if an account does not have a balance, if credit is available to the tenant, you must factor a minimum payment into the debt ratio for that account.

The property owner will define the payment amount you will use for a zero balance revolving account.

CREDIT HISTORY

E C O A	CREDITOR ACCOUNT NO	DATE RPTD	DATE LAST ACT	DATE OPND	LIMIT / HIGHEST CREDIT	PRESENT STATUS		PAY AMT	TYPE AND ACCT STATUS	HISTORICAL STATUS			
						BAL OWING	AMT PAST DUE			NO MOS HIIST REV	3 0	6 0	9 0
8	AFM-BLOOM #APRINTLO COLLECTION	02/99	04/94		425	425			OPN05				

Figure 7:12 Example - Credit Report Extract / Explanation

Type and account status will provide you with the type of account and its present status.

- Revolving   REV
- Installment   Ins
- Mortgage   Mtg
- Consumer   Cons

This field could also contain derogatory accounts such as collections, charge offs or judgments.

The number of month's history shows the numbers of months reported on the history of the account.

When you review the account, you will be seeking the status of the account.

In other words, you will review the account to determine whether the payments were made on time or if any late payment exists within the history.

You will also look for the date of each payment reference.

Minimal account history requirements may also exist.

This column will enable you to determine if the potential tenant can meet these minimum credit history requirements of the housing unit you are considering.

The historical status and late payments section provides you with numerical entries that indicate any late payments that will be found within the report.

Each account history will contain numbers indicating the status of a particular month's payment.

1 = on time

2 = 30 days late

3 = 60 days late

X = the same status as the previous month

This section of the history summary will provide you with the number of times an individual has been on time, 30 days, 60 days, and 90 days late during the reported credit history.

An account that shows a 1 indicates that the account was paid on time within the history.

When you note an account that contains derogatory information or a credit blemish, you should first confirm that the account is active and that the derogatory account is recent and the entry applies to the process.

You will then determine the last date that the account is reported and begin counting backwards from the last entry.

You will review account details by moving from left to right.

Example: Review the sample credit report included on the following
             pages.

             The reporting of this account begins in July.

             The first entry is July. Moving backwards from Left to Right the
             next entries are

             June   =   On Time
             May   =   30 Days Late
             April   =   On Time

             then backwards through time, all of the payments were
             made on time.

Example: The next account was reported in June so the backwards
             counting will begin with the month of June.

You will need to obtain an update for this account that illustrates the payment in July to bring this account current with the other entries on the report.

When you locate an account that illustrates a late payment, you will enter a 1x30 day late into the status section of your credit history-scoring key.

You will complete this process for every account in the report that contains a derogatory entry. You will export any credit blemish or derogatory entry you find on the credit report into your credit history.

Many people find it helpful to note any derogatory or important data directly on the report prior to exporting this information onto the credit history-scoring key. This helps to ensure that you do not skip any important factors during the export processes.

Increasing the Score

Over time, an individual can improve the information in his or her credit report by paying credit obligations as agreed and using credit wisely. As derogatory data in the credit report gets older, it affects the score less. A missed payment from four years ago will not count as much as a missed payment from six months ago. As the individual uses their credit in a more controlled manner, keeping debt load well below their maximum credit limits, their score is also likely to increase.

A credit score, like a credit report, is a snapshot of an individual's changing credit record. If you make a request for a second repository report to get an updated score, the score is likely to change for many reasons.

The credit items on the report are updated often, so new items are likely to have been added since the previous report. Repeatedly requesting an individual's credit report may substantially increase the number of inquiries on the repository report, which may affect the score adversely.

You can assist your potential tenants in understanding how they can improve their overall credit rating by reviewing the score factor reason codes with them an providing them with the direction that they need to use their credit wisely in the future.

Removing Erroneous Information

Consumers who want to address what they believe is erroneous information on a credit report should contact the credit repository that developed the report.

The Fair Credit Reporting Act (FCRA) allows the credit-reporting agency a "reasonable period of time", generally not to exceed 30 days, to investigate consumer disputed items.

A significant number of credit grantors use an automated system for investigating the disputes and are able to respond to a disputed item within a few days. Most credit reporting agencies make a special effort to resolve disputed information affecting a housing decision.

You will have the ability to request a credit supplement. This is typically done by completing the last page of the credit report requesting further information. Most repositories will allow you to fax the supplement request, along with the Consent for Credit Check signed by the individual who is named on the report, to the office creating the credit report.

Upon receipt of the supplement request, a staff member of the Credit Reporting Office will verify the validity and status of the debt. The staff member will issue a credit supplement. This supplement will show the true status of the account as of the date that the supplement was printed.

Because the score uses all of the credit-related data on the credit bureau report and takes into account all contributing factors, removing or changing one specific, derogatory item will not guarantee an increase in Credit Bureau Score. In some cases, a change in the credit bureau report will have little or no effect on the score. Because there are many scorecards and the score is calculated using a complex mathematical formula, it is not possible to estimate how much the score will change if specific derogatory information is removed.

MERGED INFILE CREDIT REPORT

Prepared For:	Property Address:	Prepared By:	Date Rec:
Attention:	Loan Type: Purpose of Loan: Report Type:	Computer ID: Lender Case #:	Date Comp: Date Revised:

APPLICANT	CO-APPLICANT
Name: SSN: DOB: Marital Status: Dependents: Home Phone: Present Address: Since: Own / Rent Previous Address:	Name: SSN: DOB: Marital Status: Dependents: Home Phone: Present Address: Since: Own / Rent Previous Address:

CREDIT SUMMARY

	PAYMENTS	BALANCES	LIMITS	TRADES	30+	60+	90+
REVOLVING	0	2061	2200	4	4	4	17
INSTALLMENT	1307	79365	90610	25	34	8	27
REAL ESTATE	378	35384	36600	1	2	0	0
OPEN/OTHER	991	1041	1041	5	0	0	0
TOTAL	2676	117851	129451	38	40	12	44

INQUIRIES 50   # PUBLIC RECORDS   0
BANKRUPTCIES   0   WORST TRADE   9
OLDEST DATE   07/01/89
SATISFACTORIES17

2   JUDGEMENT   RPTD – 09/96 VRFD -   OPND –

122

```
CASE – 104                              SRCE – 1011        AMT – 13245
ASSET -            LIAB -               BAL -              LACT – 09/96
                                        PLTF -                        XPN01

1    JUDGEMENT       RPTD – 11/94 VRFD -                   OPND –
     CASE – 9401                        SRCE – 1016        AMT – 1900
     ASSET -            LIAB -          BAL -              LACT – 01/95
                        PLTF -                                         XPN01
```

8   BEACON SCORE   EFX01
519
SERIOUS DELINQUENCY AND DEROGATORY PUBLIC RECORD OR
COLLECTION FILED
AMOUNT OWED ON DELINQUENT ACCOUNTS
PROPORTION OF BALANCES TO CREDIT LIMITS TOO HIGH ON
REVOLVING ACCOUNTS
LENGTH OF TIME ACCOUNTS HAVE BEEN ESTABLISHED

8   EMPIRICA SCORE   TRU01
493
SERIOUS DELINQUENCY, AND PUBLIC RECORD OR COLLECTION
FILED
LEVEL OF DELINQUENCY ON ACCOUNTS
TIME SINCE DELINQUENCY IS TOO RECENT OR UNKNOWN
        PROPORTION OF REVOLVING BALANCES TO REVOLVING
CREDIT LIMITS IS TOO HIGH

8   FAIR ISAAC SCORE   XPN01
529
SERIOUS DELINQUENCY AND PUBLIC RECORD OR COLLECTION
FILED
PROPORTION OF BALANCES TOO HIGH ON REVOLVING ACCOUNTS
NUMBER OF ACCOUNTS DELINQUENT
LENGTH OF TIME SINCE LEGAL ITEM FILED OR COLLECTION ITEM
REPORTED

CREDIT HISTORY

E C O A	CREDITOR ACCOUNT NO	DATE RPTED	DATE LAST ACT	DATE OPND	LIMIT / HIGHEST CREDIT	PRESENT STATUS		TERMS	PAY AMT	TYPE AND ACCT STATUS	HISTORICAL STATUS			
						BALANCE OWING	AMOUNT PAST DUE				NO MOS HIIST REV	30	60	90
8	AFM-BLOOM #APRINTLO COLLECTIO	02/99	04/94		425	425				OPN05				
											132111111 TRU01			
8	BENEFICL-HFC #7101702	07/00	04/00	03/97	0	0	0	39M 125		INS 01	37	0	0	0
											XX1111111X1111111111X XXX111111111111111111 TRU01			
8	CAPTIAL 1 BK 05291071382	04/00	01/00	06/96	592	0	0			REV01	41	0	0	0
											1111111111111111111111 1111111111111111111111 TRU01			
8	CCB 42270972 CREDIT CARD	07/00	02/00	07/98	950	0				REV01	24	0	0	0
											EFX01			
1	CITIBANK 54241800	06/00	06/00	12/99	3500	3516	0	72	72	REV01	8	0	0	0
											11111111 TRU01			
8	CORNER STONE S0000070010	09/00	06/96	09/94	4374	0	0	18M 223		INS00	1	0	0	0
											TRU01			
8	DIRECT MERCH BK 54580000114	07/00	07/00	11/95	2600	2496		83	83	REV01	25	0	0	0
											1111111111111111111111 1111111111111111111111 XPN01			
8	AFM-BLOOM #APRINTLO COLLEC CLOSED – CONS	02/99	04/94		425	425				OPN05				
											132111111 TRU01			
8	BENEFICL-HFC #7101702 CLOSED	07/00	04/00	03/97	0	0	0	39M 125		INS 01	37	0	0	0
											XX1111111X1111111111X XXX111111111111111111 TRU01			
8	CAPTIAL 1 BK 05291071382 CLOSED – CONS	04/00	01/00	06/96	592	0	0			REV01	41	0	0	0
											1111111111111111111111 1111111111111111111111 TRU01			
8	CCB 42270972 CREDIT CARD CREDIT CARD	07/00	02/00	07/98	950	0				REV01	24	0	0	0
											EFX01			

E C O A	CREDITOR ACCOUNT NO	DATE RPTED	DATE LAST ACT	DATE OPND	LIMIT / HIGHEST CREDIT	PRESENT STATUS		TERMS	PAY AMT	TYPE AND ACCT STATUS	HISTORICAL STATUS			
						BALANCE OWING	AMOUNT PAST DUE				NO MOS HIIST REV	30	60	90
1	CITIBANK 54241800 CREDIT CARD	06/00	06/00	12/99	3500	3516	0	72	72	REV01	8	0	0	0
											11111111 TRU01			
8	CORNER STONE S0000070010 CLOSED AUTO	09/00	06/96	09/94	4374	0	0	18M 223		INS00	1	0	0	0
											TRU01			
8	DIRECT MERCH BK 54580000114 CREDIT CARD	07/00	07/00	11/95	2600	2496		83	83	REV01	25	0	0	0
											111111111111111111111 111111111111111111111 XPN01			
1	FCNB/NEWP 4220507 CHARGE ACCOUNT	07/00	06/00	09/99	900	888		30	30	REV01	10	0	0	0
											111111111111111111111 111111111111111111111 TRU01			
3	FIRST USA BANK NA 5417623 CREDIT CARD	07/00	07/00	12/99	3000	2602	0	65	65	REV01	8	0	0	0
											11111111 TRU01			
2	FNANB 15230035125 CREDIT CARD	09/00	09/00	12/99	3000	1976		79	79	REV01	9	0	0	0
											111111111111111111111 11111 EPN01			
1	FNANB VISA 54063555013	06/00	06/00	06/98	700	0				REV01	27	1	0	0
											X112111111111111111111 EFX01			

FRAUD ALERT

1 TRANS ALERT
  TRU01
  # INQUIRIES IN LAST 60 DAYS: 04
  RECORDED INQUIRIES ALTER

1 HAWK ALERT
  TRU 01
  HAWK AVAILABLE AND CLEAR

Credit History (12 months)
Borrower

Mortgage Last 12 Months	Consumer Last 12 Months	Bankruptcy NOD/Foreclosure	Charge offs/Judgments
_____ X 30	_____ X 30	Chapter _____	# Filed _____
_____ X 60	_____ X 60	Discharge Date:	$ Amount _____
_____ X 90	_____ X 90	_____	$ to remain open _____
_____ X 120	_____ X 120	Balances: _____	$ to be paid _____
_____ Level	_____ Level	_____ Level	_____ Credit Score
			Estimated Credit

Credit History (12 months)
Co-Borrower

Mortgage Last 12 Months	Consumer Last 12 Months	Bankruptcy NOD/Foreclosure	Charge offs/Judgments
_____ X 30	_____ X 30	Chapter _____	# Filed _____
_____ X 60	_____ X 60	Discharge Date:	$ Amount _____
_____ X 90	_____ X 90	_____	$ to remain open _____
_____ X 120	_____ X 120	Balances: _____	$ to be paid _____
_____ Level	_____ Level	_____ Level	_____ Credit Score
			Estimated Credit

Figure 7:16 Sample Form – Credit History Grading

Credit History Scoring Key

You now have a better understanding of the inclusions of a credit report. You must learn to score each credit report to determine whether the potential tenant meets the guidelines for rental at your particular property. The credit history-scoring key provides a simple method of extracting necessary information from the report and organizing the information for credit rating functions.

To begin the credit scoring process, you should review the credit history-scoring key. This key will assist you and organizing the information found in the credit report into a format that you can easily use when placing the tenant.

The first item of importance in the credit report is the mortgage or rental history.

Locate the mortgage or rental payments for the potential tenant's primary residence on the report.

Review the entries within the status segment to determine if any late payments exist over the last 12 to 24 months.

If the potential tenant does not have a mortgage or rental history showing on their credit report, you will need to acquire other documentation in order to determine the residence payment history. This alternate form of verification is termed a VOR/VOM. This stands for verification of rent / verification of mortgage. A sample VOR/VOM is included later for you to review.

Consumer history is the next field you will review.

You will tally all of late payments falling into the consumer debt category. These will include personal loans, car loans, credit card debt, revolving lines of credit, nonresident mortgage loans, and any other report items that indicate the potential tenant makes monthly payments toward the payment of a debt.

In addition to reviewing the body of the report to determine the status of the payments on each account, you will need to review the section relating to public records.

The public records field will contain information relating to any bankruptcy, foreclosure, or judgment against the potential tenant.

You will typically become aware to look for these issues during the pre-application processes. The potential tenant will usually define any derogatory debt that exists within the credit profile.

You should review the dates of all derogatory entries to determine if it is within the review period of the credit report.

At times, a derogatory debt may be showing in the columns that has been discharges as part of a bankruptcy proceeding.

If an item is showing on the report as an open account but has been discharged as part of a bankruptcy proceeding, you will need to obtain a credit supplement from the credit-reporting agency verifying that the debt is fully discharged.

You may also be required to submit full bankruptcy discharge paperwork as supporting documentation.

Each property owner has different criteria concerning charge-offs. You should enter all of the information related to charge off, judgment and collection history in the total number and total account balances in the credit history-scoring key. You can then compare these entries to the requirements set by the property owner.

Any account related to a bankruptcy should be noted as discharged and left off the form.

You will complete the section of the scoring key related to accounts to be left open and the amount to be paid prior to or at the signing of the lease agreement based on the guidelines set forth by the property owner or management firm.

Some property owners allow certain charge off accounts to be left open. An example is an account that is less than $200 and over four-year old.

The final element that you will export into the credit scoring history key is the credit score.

Some property owners will use the middle of the three credit scores on a tri-merged report, while others will require you to use a specific repository score depending on which repository is considered the most complete for the potential tenant's particular area.

You should review the guideline manual created by the property owner to determine which credit score will be applicable for the potential tenant.

Before moving onto the next level of the tenant screening process, you will want to double check to determine if you have added any account into the scoring key more than one time. If you tally an account twice, it will affect the debt to income ratio of the potential tenant, may affect the overall credit placement, and could bar the potential tenant from obtaining one of the units you have available.

Once you have completed the credit history-scoring key, the elements of the key will be compared to the property owner's minimum tenant requirements to see if your potential tenant will qualify for a rental unit you have available.

Debt-To-Income

The ability to pay is the next important component of the application. The residential application provides you with information regarding work history and applicant income.

Many property owners or management firms will have guidelines regarding work history. Some will require a minimum of a two-year work history in the same field or profession. Others simply require a continuity of income showing that the tenant has a high probability of retaining employment and therefore income. This probability allows the owner to feel secure that the rental payments will be remitted on time and will continue throughout the term of the lease.

It is also important to assess the applicant's income compared to their overall debt load. It is vital that the applicant have the ability to pay their rental payments in a timely manner. The debt ratio is what will determine "how much" payment a particular applicant can afford.

Following are the two types of debt ratios that will be used:

Front-End Ratio is the gross income divided by the new rental payment.

This standard guideline is 29% but can be as high as 55% depending on the guidelines accepted by the property management firm or property owner.

Back-End Ratio is the gross income divided by the new rental payment and the minimum monthly payments from the other liabilities.

The standard guideline is 41% and can be as high as 55%.

You will use specific accounts to calculate each debt to income ratio.

Front-End Ratios use only the planned rental payment

FRONT END RATIO

New Rental Payment = $900	/	Income = $3,000	=	Front End Ratio
"Rent" $900	/	"Income" $3,000	=	Ratio 30%

Back-End Ratios use the <u>minimum</u> required monthly payments on all of the following:

Auto Loans

Student Loans

Personal Loans

Charge Cards - minimum required payments only.

Child Support

Alimony

Federal Tax Lien Repayment Schedules

Certain debt like utilities, insurance, and cell phone bills are not considered part of the debt to income ratio computations.

BACK END RATIO

Monthly Payments = $300	+	Rent = $900	=	Liabilities $1200
Total Liabilities $1200	/	Income $3000	+	Ratio 40%
"Rent + Monthly Payments" /		"Income"	=	Ratio 40%

In this scenario, your front-end is 30% and back-end is 40%. These ratios are acceptable for many management firms and property owners.

DEBT TO INCOME RATIO (DTI%)

Monthly Income

Applicant		Co-Applicant	
$_____	Base Pay/ _____	$_____	Base Pay/ _____
$_____	Commission/ _____	$_____	Commission/ _____
$_____	Other _____	$_____	Other _____
$_____	Other _____	$_____	Other _____
$_____	Total Monthly Income	$_____	Total Monthly Income

Combined Monthly Income $_____

Monthly Debt

Applicant		Co-Applicant	
$_____	Rent Payment	$_____	Rent Payment(factor only once)
$_____	Automobile Payment	$_____	Automobile Payment
$_____	Credit Card _____	$_____	Credit Card _____
$_____	Credit Card _____	$_____	Credit Card _____
$_____	Credit Card _____	$_____	Credit Card _____
$_____	Personal Loan _____	$_____	Personal Loan _____
$_____	Other_____	$_____	Other_____
$_____	Other_____	$_____	Other_____
$_____	Total Monthly Debt	$_____	Total Monthly Debt

Combined Monthly Debt $_____

Take combined debt $_____ (factor each debt only once – if it is a joint debt list under the primary income earner only) and divide by the combined income $_____. The percentage _____% is your monthly debt-to-income ratio. This number should be below the maximum set forth in the guidelines for the building or complex you have chosen for your clients.

Rental History

Rental history is also used to project the probability of an applicant fulfilling their lease terms.

Rental histories are frequently not included in a credit report.

If the rental history is not included in the credit report, it must be verified in another manner.

Verification forms are sent to the tenant's previous property owner or Property Management Company to verify the history of an account. These forms called VOM/VOR forms. This is short for verification of mortgage/verification of rent.

More and more property owners and rental management companies are placing equal or greater weights on verification of rent payments as on credit scores and employment history.

The rental history of an applicant and the reason that they are leaving a previous residence can provide vital information for your screening activities. This information can guide you in predicting the performance you can expect from that tenant during their lease term with your property or firm.

To obtain a VOR or VOM you must have the tenant complete a consent form that allows you to inquire into their history. These forms contain fill-in spaces for you to include your company information, the prospective tenants specifics as provided on the rental application and a specific inquiry into the information you desire the previous property owner or mortgage holder to confirm. The notes section of a VOR is often an important ally in determining the relationship the perspective tenant has created with his property owner through timely payments and stable tenancy.

A sample VOR is included on the following page for your review. You should familiarize yourself with the VOR so that you can quickly assess the inclusions and determine if the information provided by the tenant matches that provided when the VOR is returned.

REQUEST FOR VERIFICATION OF RENT OR MORTGAGE

Privacy Act Notice: This information is to be used by the agency collecting it or its assignees in determining whether you qualify as a prospective mortgagor under its program. It will not be disclosed outside the agency except as required and permitted by law. You do not have to provide this information, but if you do not your application for approval as a prospective mortgagor or borrower may be delayed or rejected. The information requested in this form is authorized by Title 38, USC. Chapter 37 (if VA); by 12 USC, Section 1701 et. Seq (if HUD/FHA); by 42 USC, Section 1452b (if HUD/CPD); and Title 42 USC, 1471 et. Seq., or 7 USC. 1971 et. Deq. (if USDA/FmHA).

Instructions   Lender – Complete items 1 through 8. Have applicant complete item 9. Forward directly to landlord named in item 1.
               Landlord Creditor – Please complete Items 10 through 18 and return directly to lender named in item 2.
               This form is to be transmitted directly to the lender and is not to be transmitted through the applicant or any other party.

Part I – Request

1. To (Name and address of Landlord Creditor)	2. From (Name and address of Lender)

I certify that this verification has been sent directly to the landlord/creditor and ahs not passed through the hands of the applicant or any other interested party.

2. Signature of Lender	4. Title	4. Date	6. Lender's Number (Optional)

7. Information To Be Verified

Property Address	Account in the Name of __ Mortgage __ Rental __ Land Contract	Account Number

I have applied for a mortgage loan. My signature below authorizes verification of mortgage or rent information.

8. Name and Address of Applicant(s)	9. Signature of Applicant(s) X X

Part II – To Be Completed by the Landlord/Creditor

We have received an application for a loan from the above, to whom we understand you rent or have extended a loan. In addition to the information requested below, please furnish us with any information you might have that will assist us in processing the loan.

__ Rental Account	__ Mortgage Account	__ Land Contract
10. Tenant Rented from _____ to _____ Amount of rent $_____ per _____ Number of late payments _____ Is account satisfactory? __ Yes __ No	11. Date account opened _____ Original contract amount $_____ Current account balance $_____ Monthly Payment (P&I) $_____ Payment with T&I $_____ Is account current? __ Yes __ No Was loan assumed? __ Yes __ No Satisfactory account? __ Yes __ No	12. Interest Rate _____ % __ Fixed __ ARM __ FHA __ VA __ CONV __ Other Next pay date_____ No. of late payments _____ No. of late charges _____ Owner of First Mortgage _____

Payment History for the previous 12 months must be provided n order to comply with secondary mortgage market requirements.

13. Additional information which may be of assistance in determination of credit worthiness

14. Signature of Landlord/Creditor Representative	15. Title (please print or type)	Date

Figure 7:20 Sample Form – Verification of Rent / Mortgage – HUD Release

You will enter the applicable information into section 1 and 2 of the form.

You should sign and date the form and include your title to illustrate to the mortgage holder or property owner that you are an authorized representative and therefore privy to this data.

You will enter the potential tenant's PRESENT or PAST housing address into the field property address.

The address entered should be the one whose payment history you are verifying, not necessarily the potential tenant's present address. You should have the potential tenant sign the authorization so that the individual knows that they have approved the release of their personal history.

The property owner or mortgage holder will complete part two of the form and return it to your office.

Upon receipt of the completed document, you should verify that the payment history, payment amount, and term of occupancy equate to the information entered into the tenant's application.

If there is any discrepancy between the information contained on the form and the information in the potential tenant's file, you should have the incorrect forms corrected.

Subsidized Housing

You may be working with a property owner or firm who makes units available that qualify for subsidized housing. Subsidized housing is a program that makes funds available to low or moderate-income individuals and families through a government assistance program. This program offsets some of the costs of housing for these individuals. The subsidy is paid to the Public Housing Authority and distributed to the property owner to cover some housing costs for the qualified tenants.

There are regulations regarding subsidized housing in each state. If you are working with individuals who may qualify or with a particular property that is qualified for subsidized housing funds you will want to check with your local and state authorities for specific guidelines to assist you in better understanding subsidized housing.

If you are working with a property that allows subsidized rentals or is approved as Section 8 Housing, there are some eligibility requirements that will apply to the applicants.

These eligibility requirements and the processes for payment are continuously under construction. The following information was accurate as of the time of printing, but you will want to refer to the most current guidelines for low and moderate income housing for the most accurate and up-to-date information.

- A tenant must be under the low-income level that is determined by district and is based upon national figures as applied to cost of living. Typically, the tenant must have an income lower than 50% of the median national income. This income is adjusted for family size.

- Eligible households may contain a single person, a single person who is handicapped or disabled, a displaced person or a family unit.

Subsidized housing payments are divided with the tenant paying a percentage of the rental allocation and the remainder being subsidized through the administrative agency. It is typical for the out of pocket expense for the tenant to be based upon 30% of the tenant's adjusted income. The subsidy mechanism is set up to pay the remainder portion of the contract rent on the unit directly to the property owner, manager or rental firm.

Lease applications must be taken for each applicant. These applications must be fully completed with all the pertinent information verified by the employer, government agency or banking institution that is providing subsidized housing payments for the tenants.

Bank and Employment References

The last step in completing an inquiry into the history and circumstances of a prospective tenant is the confirmation of the banking and employment references provided on the rental application. The ability to confirm the information provided on the rental application through third party sources will often provide you with the final determining factors in the screening of a potential tenant. Even when you believe the tenant is stable and your belief appears to be confirmed by the inclusions on the credit report, rental application and through the documentation provided by the tenant, it is essential that you verify information through third party references.

Earlier we showed you to complete a VOR or VOM form on each applicant. You should complete a similar inquiry into the bank account status and employment stability of the potential tenant. This verification is completed using a VOD form that you will forward to the bank reference provided by the tenant and a VOE form that you will the tenant's employer complete. VOD stands for a Verification of Deposit and VOE is Verification of Employment.

When you complete a VOD your goal is not to determine the exact balance of a potential tenant's account but to obtain verification that the account exists as the potential tenant has stated and that it is not currently overdrawn.

The VOE form will assist you in determining if the potential tenant has a stable position that will enable them to continue to meet their credit obligations as they have in the past. The VOE will provide you with the term of employment. This term should match the term listed on the rental application. The VOE will also give you the employer's opinion as to the probability of the tenant's continued employment. You will want to pay strict attention to this section. The stability of past employment is important but the likelihood that the potential tenant will remain in this position and continue to obtain the income that allowed them to meet their obligations is vital. If the potential tenant is not likely to continue in their current position and has not provided you with information regarding future income plans, it is not as likely that they will make all of their obligations on time regardless of the condition of their credit report.

REQUEST FOR VERIFICATION OF EMPLOYMENT

Privacy Act Notice: This information is to be used by the agency collecting it or its assignees in determining whether you qualify as a prospective mortgagor under its program. It will not be disclosed outside the agency except as required and permitted by law. You do not have to provide this information, but if you do not your application for approval as a prospective mortgagor or borrower may be delayed or rejected. The information requested in this form is authorized by Title 38, USC. Chapter 37 (if VA); by 12 USC, Section 1701 et. Seq (if HUD/FHA); by 42 USC, Section 1452b (if HUD/CPD); and Title 42 USC, 1471 et. Seq., or 7 USC. 1971 et. Deq. (if USDA/FmHA).

Instructions	Lender – Complete items 1 through 7. Have applicant complete item 8. Forward directly to employer named in item 1. Employer – Please complete either Part II or Part III as applicable. Complete Part IV and return directly to lender named in item 2. This form is to be transmitted directly to the lender and is not to be transmitted through the applicant or any other party.

Part I – Request

1. To (Name and address of employer)	2. From (Name and address of Lender)

I certify that this verification has been sent directly to the employer and ahs not passed through the hands of the applicant or any other interested party.

2. Signature of Lender	4. Title	4. Date	6. Lender's Number (Optional)

I have applied for a mortgage loan and stated that I am now or was formerly employed by you. My signature below authorizes verification of this information.

7. Name and Address of Applicant (include employee or badge number)	8. Signature of Applicant

Part II – Verification of Present Employment

9. Applicant's Date of Employment	10. Present Position	11. Probability of Continued Employment

12A. Current Gross Base Pay (enter Amount and Check Period) __ Annual __ Hourly __ Monthly __ Other (specify) $ _____ __ Weekly	13 For Military Personnel Only		14. If Overtime or Bonus is Applicable Is Its Continuance Likely? Overtime __ Yes __ No Bonus __ Yes __ No
	Pay Grade		15. If paid hourly – average hours per week
	Type	Monthly Amount	
	Base Pay	$	

Type	Year to Date	Past Year 20_	Past Year 20_	Rations	$	16. Date of applicant's next pay increase
Base Pay	$	$	$	Flight or Hazard	$	
Overtime	$	$	$	Clothing	$	17. Projected amount of next pay increase
				Quarters	$	
Commissions	$	$	$	Pro Pay	$	18. Date of applicant's last pay increase
Bonus	$	$	$	Overseas or Combat	$	19. Amount of last pay increase
Total	$	$	$	Variable Housing Allowance	$	

20. Remarks (If employee was off work for any length of time, please indicate time period and reason)

Part III Verification of Previous Employment

21. Date Hired	23. Salary/Wage at Termination Per (Year) (Month) (Week)
22. Date Terminated	Base _____ Overtime _____ Commissions _____ Bonus
24. Reason for Leaving	25. Position Held

Part IV – Authorized Signature – Federal statutes provide severe penalties for any fraud, intentional misrepresentation, or criminal connivance or conspiracy purposed to influence the issuance of any guaranty or insurance by the VA Secretary, the U.S.D.A., FmHA/FHA Commissioner, or the HUD/CPD Assistant Secretary.

26. Signature of Employer	27. Title (please print or type)	28. Date
29. Print or type named signed in item 26	30. Phone No.	

Figure 7:21 Sample Form – Verification of Employment – HUD Release

You will complete sections 1 through 7 of the VOE request form.

You will include the name of the employer and the applicable supervisor from whom the information is being requested.

You should enter both your name and the company name as confirmation to the employer regarding the source of the request.

Your full mailing address and any fax number that may be used for the return of the V. O. E. form should be included in the heading.

You will sign the form as verification of the source of the request.

Include your title and the date of the request.

Section 7 allows you to include the information pertaining to the potential tenant so the employer has an easy reference when completing the form.

The potential tenant should sign the form so that the employer knows that the release of the applicable employment data is authorized by the individual.

You may also attach the credit and information consent form that the potential tenant completed during the application process as additional verification that the potential tenant authorizes the release of the employment data.

The employer will complete PART 2 of the form and return it to your office.

When you receive the completed V. O. E., you should review all of the inclusions to ensure that they match the information contained within the potential tenant's application.

REQUEST FOR VERIFICATION OF DEPOSIT

Privacy Act Notice: This information is to be used by the agency collecting it or its assignees in determining whether you qualify as a prospective mortgagor under its program. It will not be disclosed outside the agency except as required and permitted by law. You do not have to provide this information, but if you do not your application for approval as a prospective mortgagor or borrower may be delayed or rejected. The information requested in this form is authorized by Title 38, USC. Chapter 37 (if VA); by 12 USC, Section 1701 et. Seq (if HUD/FHA); by 42 USC, Section 1452b (if HUD/CPD); and Title 42 USC, 1471 et. Seq., or 7 USC. 1971 et. Deq. (If USDA/FmHA).

Instructions   Lender – Complete Items 1 through 8. Have applicant complete item 9. Forward directly to depository named in item 1.
                   Depository – Please complete Items 10 through 18 and return DIRECTLY to lender named in item 2.
                   This form is to be transmitted directly to the lender and is not to be transmitted through the applicant or any other party.

PART I - REQUEST

1. To (Name and address of depository)	2. From (Name and address of Lender)

I certify that this verification has been sent directly to the bank or depository and ahs not passed through the hands of the applicant or any other interested party.

2. Signature of Lender	4. Title	4. Date	6. Lender's Number (Optional)

7. Information To Be Verified

Type of Account	Account in Name of	Account Number	Balance
			$
			$
			$

To Depository: I/We have applied for a mortgage loan and stated in my financial statement that the balance on deposit with you is as shown above. You are authorized to verify this information and to supply the lender identified above with the information requested in Items 10 through 13. Your response is solely a matter of courtesy for which no responsibility is attached to your institution or any of your officers.

8. Name and Address of Applicant(s)	9. Signature of Applicant(s)

PART II – VERIFICATION OF DEPOSITORY To Be Completed By Depository

10. Deposit Accounts of Applicant(s)

Type of Account	Account in Name of	Account Number	Balance
			$
			$
			$

11. Loans Outstanding To Applicants

Loan Number	Date of Loan	Original Amount	Current Balance	Installments (Monthly/Quarterly)		Secured By	Number of Late Payments
		$	$	$	per		
		$	$	$	per		
		$	$	$	per		

12. Please include any additional information that may be of assistance in determination of credit worthiness. (Please include information on loans paid-in-full in Item 11 above)

13. If the name(s) on the account(s) differ from those listed in Item 7, please supply the name(s) on the account(s) as reflected by your records.

PART III – Authorized Signature – Federal statutes provide severe penalty for any fraud, intentional misrepresentation, or criminal connivance or conspiracy purposed to influence the issuance of any guaranty or insurance by the VA Secretary, the U.S.D.A., FmHA/FHA Commissioner, or the HUD/CPD Assistant Secretary.

14. Signature of Depository Representative	15. Title (please print or type)	16. Date

17. Please print or type name signed in item 14	18. Phone No.

Figure 7:22 Sample Form – Verification of Deposit – HUD Release

UNDERSTANDING LEASE AGREEMENTS

9

A lease is a contract between the representative of a rental property and the tenant who plans to occupy the property. For a lease to be valid, both signing parties must be legally competent and there must be a mutual agreement concerning the terms and conditions of the lease.

The lease is the written outline of the negotiations pertaining to payment of rent and other obligations between the property owner and the tenant. The main components of the lease are:

- The names of the tenants

- The names of the property management firm or property owner

- A description of the property to be rented

- An agreement to lease the property to the tenant

- Provisions for the payment of rent

- The starting and ending dates of the lease agreement

- Signatures of all parties

These are the basic requirements of a lease. There are many additional statements and clauses that the property management firm or property owner may wish to include in the lease agreement.

There are many lease forms available for use. The following example contains the most common elements of residential rental lease. The example included is for educational purposes only. This sample has been modified from the publicly accepted and published forms offered by HUD and other regulatory agencies for use by the public in real estate transactions. You should consult the services of an attorney or real estate professional to ensure your lease agreement meets all of your needs.

Residential Lease Agreement

THIS LEASE AGREEMENT (hereinafter referred to as the "Agreement") made and entered into this _____ day of _____, 20_____, by and between

_____
(hereinafter referred to as "Landlord") and

_____

_____ (hereinafter referred to as "Tenant").

W I T N E S S E T H :

WHEREAS, Landlord is the fee owner of certain real property being, lying and situated in _____ County, State of _____, such real property having a street address of

_____
(Hereinafter referred to as the "Premises")

WHEREAS, Landlord is desirous of leasing the Premises to Tenant upon the terms and conditions as contained herein; and

WHEREAS, Tenant is desirous of leasing the Premises from Landlord on the terms and conditions as contained herein

NOW, THEREFORE, for and in consideration of the sum of _____ DOLLARS ($_____), the covenants and obligations contained herein and other good and valuable consideration, the receipt and sufficiency of which is hereby acknowledged, the parties hereto hereby agree as follows:

1. **TERM**
   Landlord leases to Tenant and Tenant leases from Landlord the above described Premises together with any and all appurtenances thereto, for a term of _____ [specify number of months or years], such term

beginning on _____, and ending at 12 o'clock midnight on _____.

2. **RENT**

The total rent for the term hereof is the sum of _____ DOLLARS ($_____) payable on the _____ day of each month of the term, in equal installments of _____ DOLLARS ($_____) first and last installments to be paid upon the due execution of this Agreement, the second installment to be paid on _____. All such payments shall be made to Landlord at Landlord's address as set forth in the preamble to this Agreement on or before the due date and without demand.

3. **DAMAGE DEPOSIT**

Upon the due execution of this Agreement, Tenant shall deposit with Landlord the sum of_____ DOLLARS ($_____) receipt of which is hereby acknowledged by Landlord, as security for any damage caused to the Premises during the term hereof. Such deposit shall be returned to Tenant, without interest, and less any set off for damages to the Premises upon the termination of this Agreement.

4. **USE OF PREMISES**

The Premises shall be used and occupied by Tenant and Tenant's immediate family, consisting of _____ exclusively, as a private single family dwelling, and no part of the Premises shall be used at any time during the term of this Agreement by Tenant for the purpose of carrying on any business, profession, or trade of any kind, or for any purpose other than as a private single family dwelling. Tenant shall not allow any other person, other than Tenant's immediate family or transient relatives and friends who are guests of Tenant, to use or occupy the Premises without first obtaining Landlord's written consent to such use. Tenant shall comply with any and all laws, ordinances, rules and orders of any and all governmental or quasi-governmental authorities affecting the cleanliness, use, occupancy and preservation of the Premises.

5. CONDITION OF PREMISES

Tenant stipulates, represents and warrants that Tenant has examined the Premises, and that they are at the time of this Lease in good order, repair, and in a safe, clean and tenantable condition.

6. ASSIGNMENT AND SUB-LETTING

Tenant shall not assign this Agreement, or sub-let or grant any license to use the Premises or any part thereof without the prior written consent of Landlord. A consent by Landlord to one such assignment, sub-letting or license shall not be deemed to be a consent to any subsequent assignment, sub-letting or license. An assignment, sub-letting or license without the prior written consent of Landlord or an assignment or sub-letting by operation of law shall be absolutely null and void and shall, at Landlord's option, terminate this Agreement.

7. ALTERATIONS AND IMPROVEMENTS

Tenant shall not alter the buildings or improvements on the Premises or construct any building or make any other improvements on the Premises without the prior written consent of Landlord. Any and all alterations, changes, and/or improvements built, constructed or placed on the Premises by Tenant shall, unless otherwise provided by written agreement between Landlord and Tenant, be and become the property of Landlord and remain on the Premises at the expiration or earlier termination of this Agreement.

8. NON-DELIVERY OF POSSESSION

In the event Landlord cannot deliver possession of the Premises to Tenant upon the commencement of the Lease term, through no fault of Landlord or its agents, then Landlord or its agents shall have no liability, but the rental herein provided shall abate until possession is given. Landlord or its agents shall have thirty (30) days in which to give possession, and if possession is tendered within such time, Tenant agrees to accept the demised Premises and pay the rental herein provided from that date. In the event, possession cannot be delivered within such time, through no fault of Landlord or its agents, then this Agreement and all rights hereunder shall terminate.

9. HAZARDOUS MATERIALS

Tenant shall not keep on the Premises any item of a dangerous, flammable or explosive character that might unreasonably increase the danger of fire or explosion on the Premises or that might be considered hazardous or extra hazardous by any responsible insurance company.

10. **UTILITIES**
Tenant shall be responsible for arranging for and paying for all utility services required on the Premises.

11. **MAINTENANCE AND REPAIR; RULES**
Tenant will, at its sole expense, keep and maintain the Premises and appurtenances in good and sanitary condition and repair during the term of this Agreement and any renewal thereof. Without limiting the generality of the foregoing, Tenant shall:

(a) Not obstruct the driveways, sidewalks, courts, entryways, stairs and/or halls, which shall be used for the purposes of ingress and egress only;
(b) Keep all windows, glass, window coverings, doors, locks and hardware in good, clean order and repair;
(c) Not obstruct or cover the windows or doors;
(d) Not leave windows or doors in an open position during any inclement weather;
(e) Not hang any laundry, clothing, sheets, etc. from any window, rail, porch or balcony nor air or dry any of same within any yard area or space;
(f) Not cause or permit any locks or hooks to be placed upon any door or window without the prior written consent of Landlord;
(g) Keep all air conditioning filters clean and free from dirt;
(h) Keep all lavatories, sinks, toilets, and all other water and plumbing apparatus in good order and repair and shall use it only for the purposes for which they were constructed. Tenant shall not allow any sweepings, rubbish, sand, rags, ashes or other substances to be thrown or deposited therein. Any damage to any such apparatus and the cost of clearing stopped plumbing resulting from misuse shall be borne by Tenant;
(i) And Tenant's family and guests shall at all times maintain order in the Premises and at all places on the Premises, and shall not make or

permit any loud or improper noises, or otherwise disturb other residents;

(j) Keep all radios, television sets, stereos, phonographs, etc., turned down to a level of sound that does not annoy or interfere with other residents;

(k) Deposit all trash, garbage, rubbish or refuse in the locations provided therefore and shall not allow any trash, garbage, rubbish or refuse to be deposited or permitted to stand on the exterior of any building or within the common elements;

(l) Abide by and be bound by all rules and regulations affecting the Premises or the common area appurtenant thereto, which may be adopted or promulgated by the Condominium or Homeowners' Association having control over them.

12. DAMAGE TO PREMISES

In the event the Premises are destroyed or rendered wholly untenantable by fire, storm, earthquake, or other casualty not caused by the negligence of Tenant, this Agreement shall terminate from such time except for the purpose of enforcing rights that may have then accrued hereunder. The rental provided for herein shall then be accounted for by and between Landlord and Tenant up to the time of such injury or destruction of the Premises, Tenant paying rentals up to such date and Landlord refunding rentals collected beyond such date. Should a portion of the Premises thereby be rendered untenantable, the Landlord shall have the option of either repairing such injured or damaged portion or terminating this Lease. In the event that Landlord exercises its right to repair such untenantable portion, the rental shall abate in the proportion that the injured parts bears to the whole Premises, and such part so injured shall be restored by Landlord as speedily as practicable, after which the full rent shall recommence and the Agreement continue according to its terms.

13. INSPECTION OF PREMISES

Landlord and Landlord's agents shall have the right at all reasonable times during the term of this Agreement and any renewal thereof to enter the Premises for the purpose of inspecting the Premises and all buildings and improvements thereon. Access will also be obtained for the purposes of making any repairs, additions or alterations as may be deemed appropriate by Landlord for the preservation of the Premises or the building. Landlord and its agents shall further have the right to exhibit the Premises and to display the usual "for sale", "for rent" or "vacancy" signs on the Premises at any time within forty-five (45) days before the expiration of this Lease. The right of entry shall likewise exist for the purpose of removing placards, signs, fixtures, alterations or additions, but do not conform to this Agreement or to any restrictions, rules or regulations affecting the Premises.

14. SUBORDINATION OF LEASE

This Agreement and Tenant's interest hereunder are and shall be subordinate, junior and inferior to any and all mortgages, liens or encumbrances now or hereafter placed on the Premises by Landlord, all advances made under any such mortgages, liens or encumbrances (including, but not limited to, future advances), the interest payable on such mortgages, liens or encumbrances and any and all renewals, extensions or modifications of such mortgages, liens or encumbrances.

15. TENANTS HOLD OVER.

If Tenant remains in possession of the Premises with the consent of Landlord after the natural expiration of this Agreement, a new tenancy from month-to-month shall be created between Landlord and Tenant which shall be subject to all of the terms and conditions hereof except that rent shall then be due and owing at

_____

DOLLARS ($_____) per month and except that such tenancy shall be terminable upon fifteen (15) days written notice served by either party.

16. SURRENDER OF PREMISES

Upon the expiration of the term hereof, Tenant shall surrender the Premises in as good a state and condition as they were at the commencement of this Agreement, reasonable use and wear and tear thereof and damages by the elements excepted.

17. ANIMALS

Tenant shall be entitled to keep no more than _____ (___) domestic dogs, cats or birds; however, at such time as Tenant shall actually keep any such animal on the Premises, Tenant shall pay to Landlord a pet deposit of _____ DOLLARS ($_____),

_____ DOLLARS ($_____) of which shall be non-refundable and shall be used upon the termination or expiration of this Agreement for the purposes of cleaning the carpets of the building.

18. QUIET ENJOYMENT

Tenant, upon payment of all of the sums referred to herein as being payable by Tenant and Tenant's performance of all Tenant's agreements contained herein and Tenant's observance of all rules and regulations, shall and may peacefully and quietly have, hold and enjoy said Premises for the term hereof.

19. INDEMNIFICATION

Landlord shall not be liable for any damage or injury of or to the Tenant, Tenant's family, guests, invitees, agents or employees or to any person entering the Premises or the building of which the Premises are a part or to goods or equipment, or in the structure or equipment of the structure of which the Premises are a part, and Tenant hereby agrees to indemnify, defend and hold Landlord harmless from any and all claims or assertions of every kind and nature.

20. DEFAULT

If Tenant fails to comply with any of the material provisions of this Agreement, other than the covenant to pay rent, or of any present rules and regulations or any that may be hereafter prescribed by Landlord, or materially fails to comply with any duties imposed on Tenant by statute, within seven (7) days after delivery of written notice by Landlord specifying the non-compliance and indicating the intention of Landlord to terminate the Lease by reason thereof, Landlord may terminate this Agreement. If Tenant fails to pay rent when due and the default continues for seven (7) days thereafter, Landlord may, at Landlord's option, declare the entire balance of rent payable hereunder to be immediately due and payable and may exercise any and all rights and remedies available to Landlord at law or in equity or may immediately terminate this Agreement.

21. LATE CHARGE

In the event that any payment required to be paid by Tenant hereunder is not made within three (3) days of when due, Tenant shall pay to Landlord, in addition to such payment or other charges due hereunder, a "late fee" in the amount of

_____ DOLLARS

($_____).

22. **ABANDONMENT**

If at any time during the term of this Agreement Tenant abandons the Premises or any part thereof, Landlord may, at Landlord's option, obtain possession of the Premises in the manner provided by law, and without becoming liable to Tenant for damages or for any payment of any kind whatever. Landlord may, at Landlord's discretion, as agent for Tenant, re-let the Premises, or any part thereof, for the whole or any part thereof, for the whole or any part of the then unexpired term, and may receive and collect all rent payable by virtue of such re-letting, and, at Landlord's option, hold Tenant liable for any difference between the rent that would have been payable under this Agreement during the balance of the unexpired term, if this Agreement had continued in force, and the net rent for such period realized by Landlord by means of such re-letting. If Landlord's right of reentry is exercised following abandonment of the Premises by Tenant, then Landlord shall consider any personal property belonging to Tenant and left on the Premises to also have been abandoned, in which case Landlord may dispose of all such personal property in any manner Landlord shall deem proper and Landlord is hereby relieved of all liability for doing so.

23. **ATTORNEYS' FEES**

Should it become necessary for Landlord to employ an attorney to enforce any of the conditions or covenants hereof, including the collection of rentals or gaining possession of the Premises, Tenant agrees to pay all expenses so incurred, including a reasonable attorneys' fee.

24. **RECORDING OF AGREEMENT**

Tenant shall not record this Agreement on the Public Records of any public office. In the event that Tenant shall record this Agreement, this Agreement shall, at Landlord's option, terminate immediately and Landlord shall be entitled to all rights and remedies that it has at law or in equity.

25. GOVERNING LAW

This Agreement shall be governed, construed and interpreted by, through and under the Laws of the Commonwealth of_____.

26. SEVERABILITY

If any provision of this Agreement or the application thereof shall, for any reason and to any extent, be invalid or unenforceable, neither the remainder of this Agreement nor the application of the provision to other persons, entities or circumstances shall be affected thereby, but instead shall be enforced to the maximum extent permitted by law.

27. BINDING EFFECT

The covenants, obligations and conditions herein contained shall be binding on and inure to the benefit of the heirs, legal representatives, and assigns of the parties hereto.

28. DESCRIPTIVE HEADINGS

The descriptive headings used herein are for convenience of reference only and they are not intended to have any affect whatsoever in determining the rights or obligations of the Landlord or Tenant.

29. CONSTRUCTION

The pronouns used herein shall include, where appropriate, either gender or both, singular and plural.

30. NON-WAIVER

No indulgence, waiver, election or non-election by Landlord under this Agreement shall affect Tenant's duties and liabilities hereunder.

31. MODIFICATION

The parties hereby agree that this document contains the entire agreement between the parties and this Agreement shall not be modified, changed, altered or amended in any way except through a written amendment signed by all of the parties hereto.

32. NOTICE

Any notice required or permitted under this Lease or under state law shall be deemed sufficiently given or served if sent by United States certified mail, return receipt requested, addressed as follows:

_____

(Property Owner Representative Name)

_____

(Property Owner Representative Address)

_____

(Tenant's Name)

_____

(Tenant's Address)

Landlord and Tenant shall each have the right from time to time to change the place notice is to be given under this paragraph by written notice thereof to the other party.

33. ADDITIONAL PROVISIONS; DISCLOSURES

_____
_____
_____
_____
_____

(Property Owner should note above any disclosures about the premises that may be required under Federal or State law, such as known lead-based paint hazards in the Premises. The Landlord should also disclose any flood hazards.)

As to Landlord or legal representative of the Landlord this _____ day of _____, 20_____.

LANDLORD:

Sign: _____ Print: _____

Date: _____

As to Tenant, this _____ day of _____, 20_____.

TENANT ("Tenant"):

Sign: _____ Print: _____

Date: _____

TENANT:

Sign: _____ Print: _____

Date: _____

The example included is for educational purposes only. This sample has been modified from the publicly accepted and published forms offered by HUD and other regulatory agencies for use by the public in real estate transactions. You should consult the services of an attorney or real estate professional to ensure your lease agreement meets all of your needs

The example lease is a standard lease agreement. Property management firms, property owners and other individuals have determined additional items that occasionally need to be addressed in the lease agreement. The following pages outline some additional clauses that you may include as part of the standard lease as well as some modified clauses that may alter the terms of the standard lease.

You may use some, none or all of these clauses at some point in your residential rental management career. Before implementing any lease agreement or adding and/or modifying clauses of the standard lease, you should consult your State Laws and Regulatory Agencies to determine the legality of each clause in your jurisdiction. The services of a real estate attorney should also be retained.

These components aid in complying with the law as well as providing specific information that helps to secure the property owner against common issues that arise during occupancy. You are not required to include many of these items in your lease agreement but some of the components may be included to offer additional protection to the property owner.

OCCUPANCY
All occupants of the apartment must be named on the lease.

This provides the property owner with the right to limit the use of the unit to the appropriate number of occupants as well as providing additional security in that the apartment will not be turned over to a sublet who has not been properly screened by the property owner or property manager.

USE
The apartment is not to be used for business purposes.

This secures the property owner against heavy foot traffic, effective changes to the condition of the apartment and allows for full compliance on the part of the property owner with local zoning laws and regulations.

ADDITIONAL RENT
The tenant agrees to pay a certain sum of money or a fee for negative or costly occurrences that are the result of an action by the tenant.

These negative or costly occurrences may include late rental payments, non-sufficient funds to cover a rental check, damages that occur to the apartment, any legal fees and costs associated with eviction proceedings or other matters specific to a particular tenant.

UTILITES
The payment of the utilities for the rental unit should be clearly outlined in the lease. Any utility costs that are to be paid by the tenant are to be noted within the agreement. If the tenant neglects a utility bill, the

property owner reserves the right to pay the bill and charge the tenant for the amount paid plus_____% interest.

This clause allows the property owner to pay any utility bills that could cause a lien against the property, and to recoup the cost of such payments plus interest in the event the property owner must spend his/her own funds to maintain the status of his deed.

LANDLORD/TENANT

It is advisable to define the term landlord/tenant in the lease agreement.

The term Landlord or Property Owner refers to all owners, agents or managers of the property.

This clause allows any person with an interest in the property or retained to perform residential rental functions in relationship to the property to act in any manner outlined under the term property owner.

Tenant refers to all occupants of the property.

This clause allows the property owner to act against or serve notice to anyone who resides in the property. In the case of multiple tenants, one may speak for all.

This allows notice and action to be served upon only one tenant rather than each occupant individually.

SECURITY DEPOSIT

The handling of the security deposit should be specifically outlined in the lease agreement.

The clause should cover the reason for the security deposit as well as the uses which the property owner may disperse the security deposit funds.

The security deposit secures the performance of the lease by the tenant. The lease should specifically refer to the use of the security deposit to offset the costs to the property owner if the tenant does not complete the lease term. The lease should also specifically note the use of the security deposit to offset costs if the tenant violates any clause in the lease and causes financial loss to the property owner. Items that could fall within this category include the non-payment of utility bills or excessive trash left in the unit upon vacancy.

The lease should specifically state that the security deposit serves as a resource of funds for repairing damages to the apartment due to unreasonable wear and tear. Any damages exceeding the amount of the security deposit will be paid to the property owner in the form of additional rent.

This clause allows the property owner to offset the costs of damages that occur because of the actions of a tenant or any guest of the tenant who damages the unit in excess of basic expected wear and tear. The use of this security deposit is allowed during occupancy as well as after the unit has been vacated.

The clause also allows the property owner to require additional funds be paid by the tenant if the costs to repair damages exceeds the amount of the deposit.

Security deposits are never used as rent unless the tenant is in default on any payment and excess security deposit exists that is not allocated to damages or wear and tear.

This clause is in place specifically in reference to the last month's rental payment. It protects against the tenant assuming that the security deposit will offset the costs of the last rental payment. If the tenant offsets the last rental payment with the security deposit, the property owner has no reserve against the costs of damages that may have occurred in the unit.

If a tenant does not move in within five days after the lease commences, the property owner may consider this default and keep the security deposit and any rent paid.

This prevents a unit from sitting empty for an extended period if the tenant does not intend to rent the unit.

This also allows the property owner to secure a new tenant and limits the amount of time the unit will be vacant and providing no income.

This also offsets the costs of securing a new tenant for the vacant unit if the lease is nullified.

Tenants will receive their security deposits minus any damages, unpaid rent, or other costs as outlined within the agreement within 30 days of the move-out date.

This clause provides the property owner with the time to determine if there is excessive wear to the property and to commence repairs to determine the exact costs that are to be paid out of the security deposit. It also allows for the clearing of the last rental payment check and a determination of the existence of unpaid utility bills that may result in a lien against the property. These bills may be paid out of the security deposit. It also outlines for the tenant when they can expect a return of the funds placed in security with the property owner.

The Landlord has the right to transfer the security deposit to a new property owner at any time and without notice to the tenant.

In case of the sale of the property or the change of a residential rental management firm, the security deposits are considered assets and would become the property of the new owner. These deposits are typically transferred as part of the settlement process and would then be administered in compliance with the terms of the lease by the new owner.

PAYMENT OF FIRST INSTALLMENT AND SECURITY DEPOSIT
Upon signing the lease, the tenant shall pay the first months rent and security deposit.

If the property owner does not approve the lease, all money shall be returned to the tenant.

If the lease is approved, the terms and condition of the lease bind the tenant.

This notice creates a requirement that a security deposit and the first month's rental payment accompany all lease agreements. It also provides the tenant with the security that if the property owner denies their lease; all monies paid will be refunded.

COMMENCEMENT OF LEASE

It is important to outline the conditions of the actions that may be taken before the date the lease agreement takes effect.

Tenant may not occupy the apartment before the beginning date of the lease unless the property owner gives permission in writing.

This protects the property owner against any injury or damages that may occur before the implementation of the lease as well as providing coverage against the use of the unit before the lease protections are in place. This use, and any damages that occur as a result, would not be offset by the lease conditions and could result in a financial loss by the property owner.

INABILITY TO GIVE POSSESSION

If the apartment is not ready for occupancy by the tenant on the beginning date of the lease, the lease is not void and the property owner will owe no damages to the tenant. The property owner will pay prorated rent to the tenant for the period of delay unless the tenant is responsible for the delay.

This protects the property owner in case of an unforeseen circumstance that delays the availability of the unit. For instance, repairs to the unit taking longer than projected.

This clause allows the lease to remain in effect and binds the tenant to the lease agreement while outlining the costs that may be incurred on the part of the property owner as well as the financial reparation that the tenant may expect in such circumstances.

It is important to note that this condition is a broadly stated condition and does not specify the amount of time the apartment may remain under lease contract without occupancy becoming available. Various areas will have specific state or judicial laws concerning the availability time line of rental housing.

NO SUBLEASE OR ASSIGNMENT
The apartment cannot be sublet without the prior written consent of the property owner.

This clause again protects the property owner against occupancy of the unit by tenants who have not been properly screened to meet the property owner's minimal requirements for rental suitability.

RULES AND REGULATIONS
The attached rules and regulations are a part of this lease.

This clause allows for specific regulations that pertain to a specific rental unit or building to be included as part of the lease agreement. For instance, if the rental has a pool or laundry facility available the lease may contain regulations pertaining specifically to the use of these facilities.

REASONABLE ACCESS
The property owner, or property management representative, has the right to enter the apartment at any time in an emergency and during reasonable hours for the purpose of enforcing the lease, examining the premises, making repairs or showing the apartment to prospective tenants or buyers.

This clause allows the property owner the right to enter his property for specific reasons regardless of the present occupant's presence. It is typical to include a specific right of notice or intent to enter to the tenant for any entry that is not the result of an emergency. This notice provides for the privacy of the tenant while maintaining the property owner's rights to inspect or act within his property.

SERVICES PROVIDED BY THE LANDLORD

If any interruption of the services specified in the lease agreement occurs, the tenant is not entitled to any compensation.

This clause protects the property owner against compensation requests for a lapse in services normally provided by the property owner.

NOTICE OF MALFUNCTION

The tenant is to notify the property owner immediately of malfunction of equipment. No repairs are to be made without the supervision of the property owner.

This clause protects the property owner against suits pertaining to a damaged or malfunctioning piece of equipment that causes a loss of the quality of life to the tenant in the event the tenant does not notify the property owner. It also provides the property owner with a means of recouping his loss in the event that a piece of equipment is permanently damaged because of the tenant's failure to notify the property owner of the malfunction.

The tenant is also instructed that they may not complete any repairs to any equipment without the supervision of the property owner.

This protects the property owner from injuries that may result from the attempt of a tenant, or person acting for the tenant to perform unauthorized repairs. This also helps prevent permanent damage to the equipment that may occur because of the actions of the tenant or another person working under the direction of the tenant. This also protects the property owner from violations in repairs conducted by an unlicensed person completed or contracted by the tenant or person acting for the tenant.

ADDITIONAL SERVICES

The property owner may provide certain voluntary services that are not required by the lease. The tenant does not have the right to demand the continuation of such services.

This protects the property owner from creating a right of expectation on the part of the tenant through his actions. Providing additional services remains voluntary.

PAYMENT FOR ADDITIONAL SERVICES

The tenant agrees to pay all bills for additional services. If the bills are not paid by the next month's due date the amount will be carried over to be paid with the following month's rent and interest in the amount of ___% may be applied.

This allows the property owner to contract for additional services with the tenant. Additional services contracted by the property owner that cannot be expected as part of the tenant's obligations cannot be charged to the tenant. Services that the property owner provides because of the tenant's inaction can be charged to the tenant. These could include the tenant not removing snow in a reasonable period. The charges incurred by the owner to remedy the situation are considered as a charge expected on the part of the tenant.

HAZARDOUS MATERIALS

Neither the tenant nor any person occupying the apartment shall bring hazardous materials into the apartment or building, nor commit any act that may effect the fire or hazard insurance of the apartment and/or building.

This clause protects the property owner against suits brought due to the action of a tenant concerning damages that may occur because of hazardous materials. It also allows for tenant responsibility in the event that a loss occurs that the property owner's fire or hazard insurance does not cover but that is a direct result of the tenant's actions.

DAMAGE OR DESTRUCTION

The tenant will use all reasonable precautions against fire or other hazards. In case of damage, there shall be no rent concessions and the property owner will repair the damage as soon as possible. If the property owner judges the damages irreparable, the lease shall terminate and the tenant will pay rent up to the time of the damage.

This clause specifically states how damage situations will be handled.

INSURANCE

The property owner is not responsible for the tenant's personal property. All tenants must carry personal property insurance coverage that will cover the damage or loss of the tenant's personal property as well as comprehensive general liability insurance with a licensed insurance company that carries a minimum of $_____ coverage against liability for bodily injury or property damage.

This clause specifically outlines the responsibility for coverage in events such as the loss of personal property or damages that may occur to a person or item in an area of the building or property that can reasonably be considered the tenant's responsibility.

TERMINATION / RENEWAL

The property owner shall notify the tenant of proposed renewal changes to the lease 75 days before the termination date of the lease.

This clause outlines the property owner's responsibility in regards to notification if there will be specific changes to the terms and conditions of the negotiated lease agreement at the time of the renewal of the lease or extensions of the lease term.

If the tenant does not notify the property owner of intent to vacate the property within ten days of receiving said renewal notice, the property owner will assume the tenant has agreed to stay for the stated renewal period.

This provides a specific period for the tenant to respond to the property owner's notice. If the tenant does not respond, this allows the property owner a reasonable expectation that the tenant intends to comply with the notice.

If no agreement to vacate the apartment or renew the lease is made by the property owner or tenant, the original lease will continue on a month-to-month basis and binds said tenant. Rent will increase 10% over the amount stated on the original lease agreement and a 30-day written notice of intent to vacate the apartment is required from either party.

This allows either the tenant or the property owner to extend the lease agreement on a month-to-month basis until a new long-term lease is negotiated or the property is vacated.

This agreement also compensates the property owner for the insecurity of a month-to-month lease by adding a 10% rental payment increase to the agreed upon sum.

SURRENDER OF APARTMENT
The tenant is required to leave the apartment in the same condition it was in upon occupancy. Normal and expected wear and tear is excluded. All keys must be returned to the management.

This clause outlines the expectations for the condition of the unit as well as the process for returning keys and other access items to the property owner or manager.

RELEASE AND INDEMNIFICATION OF LANDLORD
Property owner is relived from all claims of damage and injury.

This clause again protects the property owner from claims resulting from harm suffered by the tenant or their guests.

EVENTS OF DEFAULT
The following events shall be considered default on the part of the tenant:

Rent is not paid on time
Failure to comply with lease terms
Move out by the tenant with rent owing or full term of lease not completed

Tenant has become bankrupt or insolvent
Tenant gives false information on the application

This section outlines the items that allow the property owner to consider the tenant automatically in default of the agreement. Upon default, the tenant forfeits all monies as agreed and the property owner reserves the right to nullify the lease and begin eviction proceedings.

NO WAIVER OF PERFORMANCE

If the property owner does not require or enforce portions of the lease, the tenant is not exempt from the terms of those portions.

This protects the property owner from inadvertently creating an expectation of exception to any portion of the lease terms. In some cases, the failure to enforce a particular point or the exception to a particular point on a one-time basis or multi-incident basis can be claimed to have created an exception by example to a section of the lease.

This clause allows the property owner to make exceptions to lease terms without being in jeopardy of creating a permanent exception.

PROPERTY OWNER REMEDIES

If a breach of the lease occurs, the property owner may accelerate the lease, making the balance of the rent owed for the lease term due. This includes any legal or filing fees.

This clause outlines the property owners right to expect the full payment for the agreed upon lease term even if the tenant does not occupy or possess the unit for the entire term period.

The property owner may enter the apartment, take possession or sell the possessions of the tenant.

This gives the property owner the right to reclaim the unit in case of default without waiting for the lease term to expire.

This also gives the property owner the right to dispose of the tenant's personal property for gain in an effort to offset monies owed by the tenant.

In the event the tenant violates the conditions of the lease, the property owner has the right to consider the lease to be terminated and is under no obligation to notify the tenant of the breach or termination.

The tenant has no right to avoid such termination by compliance with the lease after the fact. The tenants may not bring themselves into compliance after the breach has occurred in an effort to avoid the property owner's termination and repossession of the unit.

Termination of the lease and recovery of the apartment does not void the right of the property owner to recover rents due, or additional charges or damages.

This clause states that the simple return of possession of the apartment does not nullify the financial debt owed by the tenant and protects the property owner's right to continue to pursue payment of the amounts owed.

Notice given by the property owner is a courtesy and not a requirement of the lease. The tenant waives the right to be given notice of a breach of any of the lease terms.

This clause allows the process of termination of the lease to be speeded and nullifies the need on the part of the property owner for notifications. The property owner may still provide notifications pertaining to breach of the agreement on the part of the tenant but this is considered an act of courtesy rather than requirement.

The expectation is that the tenant is fully aware of their actions that result in a violation of the contract conditions.

CONDEMNATION

If the whole apartment building is condemned, the lease will terminate and no more rent will be due. If only a portion of the apartment building is condemned, rent will be reduced by the percentage of square feet lost.

This clause protects the tenant in the event the entire apartment is deemed unlivable and outlines the responsibility of the property owner to provide a pro-rated rental reimbursement in the event that a portion of the apartment is deemed unusable.

The clause also protects the property owner from total loss if only a portion of their property is deemed unusable.

SUBORDINATION

The tenant agrees that the terms and conditions of the lease shall be valid even if the ownership of said lease changes.

Leases are considered as assets when the ownership of rental real estate changes.

This clause allows for the sale of property leases and the transfer of payments received from the leases to the new owners.

AGENT

The agent is acting only as an agent and is not liable to the tenent or property owner for the fulfillment of the lease terms.

This applies in the event an agent is used for the management or leasing of a rental unit.

The clause protects the agent from liability for any part of the lease agreement or the breach of the agreement by the property owner or the tenant.

LEASING BROKERAGE

The property owner agrees that the agent my procure the lease, possess the lease, collect rent payments and deposits and be paid a lease commission.

This clause outlines the position, responsibilities and payment arrangements for the property manager.

INSPECTION OF PREMISIS
The tenant has the right to inspect the apartment before taking possession and the tenant must schedule a time for the inspection. The property owner is not responsible for altering the apartment at the signing of the lease.

This clause allows the tenant the right to inspect the condition of the apartment prior to occupation to determine that the apartment is as expected and note the condition of the apartment in case of any dispute concerning damages that may occur.

This clause also protects the property owner from the expectation of alterations that the tenant may deem desired. The tenant is given no rights to expect any alterations to the property other than those stated in writing at the time of lease signing.

CONDUCT OF TENANT
During the occupancy of the apartment, the tenant will take care of the apartment and any appliances included.

Damage by the tenant due to misuse or neglect by the tenant will be repaired by the property owner and paid for by the tenant.

This outlines the tenant's obligation to care for the property of the property owner in a reasonable manner and to be responsible for the cost of any repairs that are required because of the misuse or neglect on the part of the tenant.

DEATH OR PERMENANT INCAPACITATION OF TENANT

If the tenant dies, any agent for the property owner or tenant can terminate the lease by giving two months notice.

This allows for the termination of the lease and repossession of the unit by the property owner in the event the tenant who signed the lease becomes permanently incapacitated or dies. This also allows a 60-day time within which the agents of the tenant may remove the tenant's personal property.

NOTICE

All notices given to the tenant by the property owner may be left at the apartment.

This allows the property owner to serve notice at the apartment unit covered in the lease regardless of the actual current location of the tenant.

All notices given by the tenant to the property owner must be delivered by either certified or registered mail to the address of the owner or the address of the management office as outlined within the lease.

This clause outlines the only accepted method of delivery of notices on the part of the tenant, providing a third-party confirmation of delivery in case of a dispute.

SIGNS

Tenants may not place any signs on the property.

This clause protects the property owner's right to maintain an acceptable appearance of their property at all times.

PETS

No pets are allowed unless specifically approved in writing by the property owner.

This clause allows the property owner to determine the suitability of a proposed pet and either accept or deny the right of the tenant to maintain the pet on the property owner's property and to specify the conditions under which a pet may be maintained.

CREDIT APPROVAL

The property owner's approval of tenant's credit is based upon the report given by the credit bureau.

SEVERABILITY

Any portion of the lease that is found invalid will affect only that portion of the lease and has no effect on the remainder of the lease.

This clause protects the conditions of the lease and the property owner's ability to enforce all remaining conditions if one condition is found to be against a housing law on a judicial, state or federal level.

ENTIRE AGREEMENT

The terms and conditions of the lease are written in the lease and in the rules and regulations.

NO verbal agreements will pertain to the lease.

Any changes or alterations to the lease document must be written and signed by both the property owner and the tenant.

This clause protects against either party claiming a verbal agreement is binding and allows for the speedy resolution of all disputes. It provides that neither party can claim an agreement has been reached unless the agreement is outlined in writing and both parties have signed the agreement.

SECURITY DEPOSITS

The Landlord Tenant Act provides specific regulations regarding the handling of the Security Deposit. The tenant MAY NOT waive these conditions.

The current regulations are outlined below:

- The Act applies only to residential property.

- The Act applies only to security deposits of more than $100.

- The Act states that during the first year of the lease the security deposit may not total more than two months rent.

- The Act states that after the first year of the lease the security deposit may not be more than one month rent.

- The Act states that after the second year the security deposit must be placed in an interest bearing account in an approved depository.

- The Act states that the tenant must be paid the interest earned on his or her deposit every year on the anniversary of the date of the lease.

- The Act states that the property owner may deduct from the interest payment 1% of the amount of the deposit to offset the cost of administering the account.

- The Act states that the property owner may put up a bond instead of carrying an escrow account. The bond must guarantee that the tenant will get his deposit back at the time of lease termination, plus interest but less the cost of any repairs as outlined in the lease.

- The Act states that after the tenant has been in possession of the apartment for five or more years the security deposit may not be increased even in the event the rental payment amount is increased.

- The Act states that whenever the landlord puts a security deposit in any escrow account he must notify the tenant in writing and provide the name and address of the institution in which the funds were deposited as well as the amount of the deposit.

- The Act states that if the property owner fails to provide a list of damages and the balance of the deposit amount with-in 30 days of move-out the tenant is due twice the amount of the deposit.

LEASE END

Lease Assignment
An assignment is the total transfer of a lessee's rights and obligations to another person.

Sublet
A sublet is the transfer of only a portion of the rights of the lessee. The sublet assignee or subleases will typically pay rent to the lessee, who then makes rental payments to the lessor or property manager /owner.

Expiration
Many leases terminate because of the expiration of the lease.

Mutual Nullification
The property owner and the tenant may reach a mutual decision to nullify the lease. This may occur for a variety of reasons, but in essence the tenant surrenders the property to the property owner and the lease becomes invalid. This nullification should be done in writing to protect both parties.

Eviction
At times, an eviction process may become necessary. If a tenant fails to fulfill lease agreement obligations such as paying rent in a timely manner or other matters that violate the terms of the lease, the property owner has grounds to begin an eviction process.

Eviction typically occurs because of the tenant's failure to pay rent as agreed. Eviction may also be caused by other violations such as bringing animals into a no pet allowed apartment, allowing occupancy by people not named on the lease agreement, or conducting an illegal activity within the apartment for which the owner is placed in jeopardy.

Actual Eviction
An Actual Eviction process begins with the property owner serving notice on the tenant requiring the tenants to bring themselves into compliance with the lease agreement or to vacate the premises.

If the tenants do not bring themselves into compliance or vacate the premises, the property owner would then proceed with the matter in a court.

If the property owner wins the case, the court will order a termination of the tenant's lease rights. The court will typically order a sheriff or marshal to go to the rental unit and force the tenant out of the property thereby returning rights to access of the property to the owner.

Constructive Eviction
A constructive eviction occurs when the property owner does not keep the property in adequate condition for the tenant to continue occupancy.

INVESTMENT PROFIT POTENTIAL 10

There are many sound reasons for investing in rental real estate. The financial reasons for a property owner's decision to invest in real estate must be understood by the property management team. This understanding of the premise behind profit in rental real estate allows the property manger to perform their job functions in a more effective manner.

The primary objective of real estate investment is a return on that investment. This return may come in the form of cash flow, appreciation in value, equity build-up or tax benefits.

Cash Flow

A cash flow is the term used to describe the situation where the money taken in exceeds the expenses incurred by a property and the required reserves.

The cash flow is computed by taking the Gross Operating Income or GOI and deducting the expenses incurred to reach the cash flow figure.

GOI   –   Expenses   =   Cash Flow

Some properties will show a negative cash flow. If a negative cash flow occurs, the owners must fund this deficit to ensure that all expenses are paid.

The goal with any investment property is to create either a flat or a positive cash flow by computing the needed expenses, creating a system of reserve allocation that allows funds to be available for unexpected expenses, and then setting the rental requirements accordingly.

When creating a cash flow assessment it is vital that a vacancy allowance, or projection of expected vacancy rates of the available units, be included.

You will be privy to the obvious GOI and the expenses that you see on a day-to-day basis. It is important that you also remember the probable mortgage expenses that will influence the bottom line. Many property managers never view the mortgage expense and may believe that the property is performing well when it is actually operating at a loss. Any loss will directly influence the decisions the property owner makes regarding any action that you wish to take with regard to upkeep, upgrades, marketing, and other property related matters.

Appreciation

Appreciation occurs when the amount of the value of the property increases between the time the property is bought and the present.

Two forms of appreciation occur.

Forced Appreciation
Forced Appreciation is an increase in value that occurs because of action taken by the owner of the property or his agent.

Forced appreciation will occur through improvements made to the property or with management expertise that increases the rentability of the property.

Market Appreciation
Market appreciation occurs due to a property because of changes in the marketplace.

The purchase of a piece of real estate in an area that is not in a decline will typically result in some form of appreciation.

The goal of any investor in real estate is to secure the highest level of market change appreciation possible by purchasing real estate in areas that will undergo high growth in desirability, and therefore high growth in property value.

Equity Build-Up

Equity is the difference between the value of the property and the claims against the property.

Equity build up occurs when the debts secured against the property are paid down or paid in full.

The best method of equity build up in rental real estate is to use the rental income received to pay down the debts against the property. This allows the owner of the real estate to create equity using other people's money and limits the investment of their own funds that must be used for the property to a minimal amount.

Equity build up may result from either appreciation or an increase in property value and mortgage reduction or the amount of mortgage payments that go toward the loan balance.

Leverage

Leverage is the use of borrowed funds to purchase or maintain real estate. The use of leverage contributes to capital growth and the overall attractiveness of investing in real estate.

Capital Growth

Capital growth is best realized upon the sale of a property. When considering the sale of a property, investors will want to take into account the tax ramifications. Taxes can affect the amount of capital growth realized from a given property.

Tax Benefits

Another method of earning a return on investment is by using the tax benefits that have been created to make real estate investment more desirable to an investor. These tax benefits change depending on the current economic environment and tax regulations. You will want to review the current tax regulations relating to real estate investing to gain a better understanding of the tax benefits that may be realized by the property owner.

Interest

Interest paid on a mortgage is typically tax deductible.

The interest expense paid on the mortgage of an investment property is usually tax deductible. This deduction makes the burden of a mortgage easier for most investors to bear and is an element the property owner will review carefully when obtaining new rental property for the management firm to handle.

Expenses

Many basic expenses associated with a rental property are tax deductible for the property owner. The property owner will probably be able to obtain credit for property tax payments, utilities, depreciation, some renovation work and even the services of some contractors. It is vital that the property manager keeps solid records and receipts for all expenses so that the property owner can achieve the full tax benefit from the property.

Depreciation

Another deduction occurs through depreciation. Depreciation is also known as cost recovery. It is the loss a tax preparer can declare by assuming that an asset has wasted away. An important point to remember is that land cannot be depreciated; only the improvements qualify for depreciation. You may not depreciate a primary residence.

Depreciation is used only for investment property.

Depreciation occurs over a period called the recovery period. Property owners are allowed to deduct a certain percentage of the value of a property from their gross income each year. This ability to deduct a percentage of the value depreciation of a property each year benefits the government in that it encourages an investor to hold onto a property for a longer time in an effort to obtain full depreciation. There are various depreciation methods available for use.

Straight Line Depreciation

One may use a straight-line depreciation. In straight-line depreciation, an equal amount is taken as a loss for each year of the recovery period.

Straight-line depreciation is the most common form of depreciation used by investors.

In straight-line depreciation, you take the value of the wasting asset and divide it by the years in the recovery period allowed by tax law.

Example: If you have an apartment building purchased by an investor that cost $356,000 with the land value totaling 20% of the overall cost of the property you would immediately remove the land value since land is not a depreciable asset.

365,000   -   20%   =   284,000

That leaves $284,800 in assets that can be depreciated over the recovery period.

For this example, say the recovery period is 25 years.

You would divide the depreciable asset by 25 years for a yearly depreciation of $11,392.

284,000   /   25   =   11,392

This depreciation loss can be taken as a deduction each year of the recovery period on the tax return.

Because it is straight-line depreciation, the depreciation remains stable each year of ownership or until the recovery period has been reached.

Accelerated Deprecation

Accelerated depreciation provides that the loss taken shall be greater in the early years of ownership than in later years.

Accrued Depreciation

The last term is accrued depreciation. Accrued depreciation is the sum total of all depreciation taken over a number of tax years.

Tax Shelter

Using real estate as a tax shelter is one of the potential benefits to the investor.

A tax shelter provides the ability to offset the income from an investment through the employment of allowable deductions generated by that investment.

A tax shelter provides income tax savings for its owner. We have reviewed some of the tax deductions that may be taken It is important to understand that the owner who is seeking long-term appreciation rather than a monthly cash flow from the investment might create a scenario in which the monthly receipts are completely offset by the monthly expenses of the property.

The gross operating income is reduced by the subtraction of all operating expenses, interest paid on the mortgage and the depreciation of the property.

Many items will be deducted by the investor at the completion of the tax return. The easiest to understand is the depreciation allocation.

Example:	All receipts from a rental property total	$ 6750.00 monthly
	All expenses from a rental property total	$ 3155.00 monthly
	Positive monthly cash flow total	$ 3595.00 monthly
	End of year positive cash flow	$43140.00 yearly

This might appear to be a positive cash flow; however, depreciation may be allocated in addition to the cash expenses reflected by your records.

Property value less land base	$385,000.00
Depreciation allocation	29.5 years
Yearly depreciation allowance	$ 13,050.85

This allowable deprecation figure is deducted from the positive cash flow reflected within your records. The newly calculated positive income would total $30,089.15. This figure is approximately 30% of the overall income you had reflected on your books. This 30% decrease in income is a tax benefit for the investor, as he will not be required to pay income tax on this deducted portion of the income. It is important that you understand that additional calculations will occur beyond what you review in the monthly ledgers that will influence the investor's profitability in the investment.

Capital Gains Tax
When selling an investment property one of the considerations is the tax ramifications. Computing the capital gains tax for the sale of an income producing property is the same as for any other real estate except the amount of accrued depreciation or depreciation percentage taken to date.

The amount of accrued depreciation must be subtracted from the purchase price when computing the adjusted basis.

ANALYSIS WORKSHEET

Date: _____ Address: _____

Asking Price: _____ Type of Property: _____

Appraised Value: _____ Offer Analysis: _____

Financing

Total Offer Price: _____ Seller Concession: _____

Assumed Loan: _____ Payment: _____

1st Required: _____ Payment: _____

2nd Required: _____ Payment: _____

	%					Comments
Gross Income						
- Vacancy						
+Rental Income						
+ Other Income						
=Gross Operating						
- Operating Expense						
Accounting & Legal						
Advertising						
Licenses & Permits						
Insurance						

Management Fees						
Other payroll						
Benefits						
Real Estate Taxes						
Repairs						
Maintenance						
Supplies						
Utilities						
Electric						
Heating						
Water & Sewer						
Telephone						
Other						
Other Costs						
TOTAL OP EXPENSE						
NET INCOME						
- Total Debt Load						
= Pre-Tax Cash Flow						

Case Study

Date: July 7, 2004

Property Address: 112 Great Rental Lane, Any City, USA

Property Type: 3 Unit, 2 BR/1Bath Each Walk-Up

Asking Price: $48,500

Appraised Value: $49,000

Assumable Loan: $44,500

1st Required: $0

2nd Required: $ 4,500

Seller Concession: $ 3,000

Rental Income/Term:

Unit 1: $550.00/Month   Yearly through 1/2005
Unit 2: $500.00/Month   Month-to-Month
Unit 3: $450.00/Month   yearly through 6/2005

Vacancy Allowance: Assume 7%

Utilities: Water/Sewer paid by owner.
                                      All remaining utilities paid by tenant.

Misc.:   No management costs or maintenance reserves
                                      Estimated depreciation: $1750.00/year
                                      Monthly assumed payment: $ 365.00/month
                                      Yearly property taxes: $ 745.00/year
                                      Yearly Insurance: $ 394.00/year

All renovation, management and maintenance completed by the owner/operator.

Once an investor has assessed the property, determined the profitability and chosen to make a purchase the next step is to generate property budgets. As with any business a clearly outlined budget will assist the real estate investor in maintaining profitability and will act as a guide as to what actions may and may not be taken on a property at a given time.

A property owner should create two different types of budgets. These are the annual budget and the long-range budget

Each budget will contain similar components. These include:

Expected Income

Operating Expense

Finance Expense

Capital Reserve Accumulation

Owner's cash flow needs

Understanding Income-Budget

The investment property is valuable in terms of the income or cash flow generated through the rental of the property units.

To compute the actual property income:

Begin with the gross income:

Rental Units   x   Rent Received   =   Gross Income

Subtract vacancy rates and bad debt:

Gross Income   x   Vacancy %   =   Vacancy Loss

Gross Income- Vacancy Loss – Bad Debt   =   Projected Income

Subtract other costs:

Projected Income -   Other Costs   =   Total

Add additional income expected:

Total Projected Income +Other Income   =   Effective Income
(vending laundry, parking, etc.)

Operating Expense

The operating expense is the amount it will cost the investment owner to operate the rental property each month of ownership. Items that will be considered in the property expense will include:

Regular maintenance costs

Wages of the property management and other employees

Employee benefits

Fees paid to accountants and legal service providers

Property Insurance costs

Annual Real Estate Tax payments

Advertisements and promotions to secure tenants

Licenses, permits and other county costs

Expected repair and/or renovation costs

Operating supplies

Property owner paid utilities

among others

To obtain the expected operating expense figure you should determine both the monthly and yearly-expected cost of each item. Additional items may apply to a particular investment property and some items listed may not be applicable. Each expense that will be born by the investment property owner should be considered as part of the operating expense.

These figures will be analyzed by the year for budgeting. The figures obtained must also be broken down to a monthly cost analysis figure to assist the property owner in determining both cash flow and potential cash reserve needs.

A further consideration when determining cash flow and operating expenses will be to assess the tax benefits of each expense. Deductible expenses will affect the overall profitability in a different manner than those expenses that are not deductible. Likewise, deductible cash expenses will affect profitability in a slightly different way than deductible non-cash expenses. In order to clarify the impact and the allocation methods you must gain a knowledge base regarding the method that expenses are allocated by the Internal Revenue Service. You can review all rental real estate related regulations and guidelines on the IRS Website. These instructional manuals are continuously updated and amended so it should become a regular part of your continuing education to review these manuals. To assist you in better understanding what will be included in these instructions we will break down the categories you will encounter.

Deductible Non-Cash Expenses

When we say deductible non-cash expenses, we are discussing expenses that occur without requiring an actual cash payment out of the investor's pocket. These deductions benefit the investor because they lower the gross income but do not require the investor to reduce the cash in hand received from the property.

Depreciation is perhaps the most common non-cash expense the investor will assess when completing their tax return or cash flow assessment.

The depreciation on the value of a property is a standard deduction used in investment real estate. This depreciation calculation is based upon the value of the property itself. The value of the land on which the investment sits is not a depreciating asset. To calculate the standard depreciation deduction you would use the following formula.

Fair Market Value -   Land Value   =   Depreciable Base

Depreciable Base /   Allowed Years   =   Yearly Deduction

The IRS sets standard depreciation factors for the allowed year's calculation.

Deductible Cash Expenses

As we explained earlier, some of the costs involved with the ownership and operation of a rental property are deductible expenses for the property owner. These payments are actual cash expenses created through the ownership and actual operation of the rental units. It is important that you keep all records, receipts and contracts for any item that is paid by your firm on behalf of the property owner. These records will be essential to the property owner at tax time when the final cash flow assessment is completed. There are many examples of deductible cash expenses generated from investment real estate; however, the most common are property taxes, mortgage interest, legal fees, insurance premiums, vehicle expenses, some contractor services and repair costs. You should retain records of every expense regardless of your determination of deductibility. T his will allow the property owner to achieve the full tax benefits from the property.

Non-Deductible Expenses

It is important for the property manager to understand and keep records of all expenses that might benefit the property owner. However, it is equally important that adequate records be available for those expenses that must be borne by the income generated by the investment property. The tax benefit of investment real estate is vital to the property owner, but the bottom line cash flow can be equally important. It will often be a part of your position to review the base numbers on a monthly or quarterly basis.

Most property owners require that a particular investment operate within a budget to ensure that the income is adequate to meet the expenses of that property. Even when your position does not require that you oversee these figures, it is important that you understand the cash flow of the property you are managing. If a property consistently operates at a loss, the property owner might choose to sell the property, alter the operation of the investment or even remove you from your position in an attempt to balance his income and expense scenario.

Understanding Capital Reserves

Capital reserves are very important to successful property management. A strong capital reserve account will assist the property in remaining active despite periodic setbacks, excessive costs above estimates and other capital drains not planned in the monthly budget.

The property owner will need to determine what items may require a cash reserve over the life of the investment.

Example: Turn over repairs, regulated maintenance, and extended vacancy.

The property owner will need to determine how much of each month's income will be set aside toward reserves. To do so, the property owner will analyze the specifics of the property. He will:

Estimate the life of the investment ownership.

Estimate the costs of the items that may require a cash reserve with inflation considerations.

Divide the total costs assessment by the expected life of the investment.

Divide the sum by 12 (12 months in a rental year)

The total is the funds that must be held in reserve monthly to meet potential cash reserve needs.

Finance Expense

Some investors have mastered alternate methods of obtaining investment property that does not include a financing need. These might include purchases that require a small cash investment for the obtainment of the property such as Tax Sales and Foreclosure purchases. These types of purchases will typically not carry a finance expense. Other investors will take an approach that requires a certain amount of the purchase price of the property to be financed through a third party. These potential finance sources could include Conventional Finance, Assumed Loan Finance, or Seller Finance among others.

Any time a financial obligation is secured against the property the cost of that obligation should be considered as part of the property budget analysis. The actual payment toward the principal of a mortgage is often the largest non-deductible cash expense that you will note with regard to a particular investment property.

Financing will usually contain an allowance for the payment toward the principal amount owed against the property as well as payment of interest. Interest payments compensate the individual holding the mortgage against the property.

The interest portion of the monthly mortgage expense will typically be a tax-deductible cash expense. The investor will determine what portion of the payment applies toward the principal and what applies toward the interest accumulating on the balance owed. It is important for you to understand that the payment will be broken down and deducted differently at tax time. In many instances, the investor wants all expenses to be considered within the cash flow analysis regardless of the potential deduction they might obtain at tax time.

Any portions of the monthly payment that are escrowed toward the payment of the annual taxes and property insurance due on the investment will not be calculated as part of the finance expense. These are considered operating expense figures and the investor must be certain these costs are not accounted twice in the budget calculations since they can dramatically alter the budgeting results and cause a potentially profitable investment to appear to be less profitable.

Owner Needs

The last consideration when planning a budget analysis is the owner's needs. Many real estate investors operate their investment portfolio as an actual career. When the investment portfolio is intended to generate an actual income for the investor, the income needs of the owner must be considered. The income needs will actually be assessed first on a yearly basis. To begin the process of assessing the minimum required income the investor will tally all potential personal costs accumulated on a yearly basis. These will include any cost of living incurred by the investor on a personal basis. This calculation will not assess any costs incurred because of the investment property. The costs of the investment property are analyzed separately. Some items that the investor will wish to include in the yearly needs assessment are:

Housing costs of the primary residence

Utility costs at the primary residence

Personal homeowner's insurance costs

Annual taxes due on the primary residence

Allowance for food, personal purchases and entertainment expense

Health insurance for the investor and his family

Automotive payments for personal use vehicles

Credit card and other debt payments

Any debt owed by the investor

Most individuals assess their debt load on a monthly basis. For assessing the owner income needs, the monthly budget will be converted to a yearly budget need.

Monthly Expense   x   12 months   =   Yearly Need

The investor will then take their yearly cash need and divide that need by the number of investment properties owned. Each subsequent investment property purchase will alter this calculation.

Yearly Cash Need / # of Properties   =   Cash Needed Per Property

The investor will then take this cash needed on a yearly basis per property and analyze the cash requirements against the net income generated by each property. If a shortfall exists, the investor will need to determine potential remedies available to them.

The investor may expand his portfolio to add additional cash producing units in an effort to lower the cash needs requirements from each investment currently owed.

Example 1: Cash Requirement per Year $36,000 yearly
            / Investments unit's owned   /   6 units
            _____   _____
            = Cash needs per unit $ 6,000 yearly

If the investor purchases additional units, the cash needs are distributed among the total units owned. This helps to lower the needs from each individual unit.

Example 2: Cash Requirements per Year $36,000 yearly
            / Investment units owned   /   9 units
            _____   _____
            = Cash needs per unit $ 4,000 yearly

Each investment purchased by the investor must have the ability to meet all expenses required by the investor. A unit with high value against the sales price may not be a positive investment for that particular investor if the unit is unable to meet the cash flow requirements necessary for positive operations.

Some investors enter the investment arena in an effort to build real estate equity against some future financial need. These investors will typically not need a monthly or yearly cash flow for the maintenance of the investor's debt load. This type of investor may not be as concerned with the income allocation of the property against the potential expense. More frequently, investors wish to generate an immediate cash flow while building equity. When this is the case, the investor must consider each factor when assessing the property, not just the potential equity obtained by negotiating a low sales price/high-appraised value transaction.

Record Keeping

Often, the Property Manager will be the most involved in the daily operation of a rental unit or complex. This means that many of the record keeping responsibilities will fall to the Property Manager to complete and supply to the property owner in the form of reports. You reviewed an Analysis Worksheet earlier in the manual. This form is an excellent location for the final figures gathered through the records you will keep, however, you must keep records on a daily basis to assist you in determining what figures will be entered into this form.

Record keeping is a task that must be integrated into your workday. It is important to keep track of all matters that influence the financials of the rental property as they occur. It may seem simpler to complete all records on a weekly or even monthly basis since those are common time frames for the remittal of these records to the owner of the property. This delay can create many issues in the proper tracking of income and expenses. Many times, a record that is not immediately entered into the bookkeeping is forgotten, entered incorrectly or allocated to the wrong form or column. It is a best practice to integrate the entry of all records into you daily task list. This not only keeps the records more concise, it ensures that you will not fall behind on the record-keeping portion of your position.

Many individual owners report their income and pay the tax allocation on a 'cash' basis. To report on a cash basis means that they report income and deduct expenses within the period that they are paid. The cash method of accounting makes it vital that the records are kept up to date. If a billing is incurred in December but the payment for the billing is not made until the following February, the owner may not deduct the expense in the tax return year ending December 31. He will have to allocate that expense to the following year's return. When keeping records, this method of accounting requires that you enter two separate items in relationship to each expense. These are the billing date and the payment date. It is critical to the proper compliance with Tax Regulations that expenses are allocated correctly. The property owner relies heavily on your records to determine what expenses to allocate to each tax year.

The property owner will often compare the expected rental payment receipts against the bank deposits that you make for him. This provides a quick check method to locate potential cash flow issues quickly. If a portion of your position is to make the daily or weekly deposit for the investor, you should follow some basic rules to ensure that the records are easily reviewed and that all income is clearly defined.

Designate Rental vs. Other Income

You will receive different types of payments and these payments should be designated by type within your records. A good method of designating the types of income you receive is to create an accounting log that shows every receipt and provides a location for the type of income classification for each.

Example: If you receive funds for rent those would be designated as "rent – month – unit #" within the receipts log.

Example: If you receive funds from other sources such as a security deposit, payment for a service such as lawn care provided on the tenant's behalf or for another reason, you should enter these into the record journal in the most specific method possible. "reimbursement – unit # - lawn services paid for tenant – see notice regarding lack of maintenance"

Designating the type of payment received allows the investor to allocate all income for easy tax calculation and cash flow assessments.

Another consideration that should be addressed under designation is the deposits you may make on behalf of the investor. When creating deposits, you should separate the funds into two separate categories, or more if a part of the money is from a specific source that you feel should be separated. An example of a special purpose category would be the security deposit paid by the tenant. The landlord will typically have a separate account for these security payments, if not, it is a best practice to designate all security deposits and to make the deposit of each of these payments separate from all other deposit funds.

Rental funds

Other money received

Special purpose funds

Depositing each payment using a separate transaction allows for easy correlation between the record that you will keep and related bank statements.

Fixed Vs. Variable Expenses

As we explained earlier, different expenses must be addressed in a specific manner. Some expense will be deductible and some will not qualify under the IRS guidelines. Another factor that the investor will review is the type of expense allocations that exist concerning a specific investment property. These are commonly termed fixed and variable expenses.

A fixed expense is an expected cost associated with the property that stays relatively stable from one year to the next.

A variable expense is an expense that is not expected to stay stable and will alter based on the specific needs of the property in any given period.

A stable or fixed expense would include items like the mortgage payment or insurance premiums.

Variable expenses include any payment that is not regular and premium based like property repairs.

You will record fixed and variable expenses within your records. Be aware that if a cash-flow issue exists, in other words, the property income and expense balance does not meet the investor's expectations, the variable expenses will be the ones that are most closely scrutinized.

The investor will always attempt to minimize the variable expenses that are non-deductible cash expenses first when attempting to generate a higher cash flow from the investment.

Cash Flow Versus Profit

It is important that you understand that cash flow and final profitability will not be the same. Any business requires the careful assessment of all reports, including income and expenses, careful planning and excellent management to ensure that all areas of the business operate smoothly. Most people mistakenly believe that cash flow and profit figures provide the same information. However, the two are very different and are composed of a variety of components. We have provided extensive information regarding deductible vs. non-deductible expenses. You have also reviewed specifics regarding cash and non-cash expenses. These items affect the profitability of a rental property from the perspective of the investor. Each item reviewed will affect the figures that are commonly termed tax-based profitability. The property manager will typically review the raw figures entered into their records on a regular basis. However, a positive cash flow shown on the books within the rental office will sometimes reflect a negative figure when the investor completes the yearly analysis for the purpose of the tax return.

In general, most investors desire that the rental property show a flat or positive cash flow. A flat cash flow is one where the income generated matches the expenses created. This allows the property to be self-supporting and ensures that the investor is not required to feed additional funds derived from another source into the property.

The goal of many investors is to generate positive appreciation growth in the investment while creating a tax shelter scenario.

RENT

11

There are several methods that are useful in setting the rental amount expected for a given property or rental unit. The owner of the property will typically set the rental income requirements. You will use the marketing techniques and tenant screening process to assist the investor in attaining the goals they have set. The investor will often determine the type of lease. You must understand the types of payments commonly encountered within the lease agreement and ensue that you have the skills necessary to meet the income requirements created by the investor. The most common rental payment you will encounter is that designated by the gross lease.

Gross Lease
A gross lease allows the tenant to pay the property owner a fixed amount of rent each month or period.

The property owner then pays all of the expenses of the property.

A tenant who pays 350 monthly for a 1-bedroom apartment and a tenant who pays 7500 yearly for the use of a 2-bedroom house are both paying fixed rent on a gross lease.

This rental charge is a typical method for property owners and tenants when the lease term is month-to-month or yearly. If a tenant desires a longer-term lease period of 2, 5, even 10 years, the rental costs are sometimes handled in a different manner.

Step Up or Graduated Lease

A step-up or graduated lease may be negotiated between the property owner and the tenant. In this method, the rental payment is negotiated to increase in a graduated manner at certain times.

Example: A tenant who wishes to sign a 5-year lease may pay 350 per month for the first year, 375 for the second year, 400 for the third and fourth years and 425 monthly in the fifth year.

This allows the property owner to compensate for increased expenses and the tenant to secure a long-term lease with a guaranteed rental payment for the term.

REPORTS AND NOTICES 12

The collection of rental payments will be an integral portion of your position. Rental payments are the driving force of the business and must take a priority over many other duties. You may collect other monies during the completion of your duties. Some of the items and the applicable notices pertaining to these items are included on the following pages.

The notices included in this chapter are for example purposes only. The actual forms you may be required to use may vary from those included. You should check Regional and State laws and regulations and verify the applicable forms with your firm or property owner. When creating a form for use in your property management duties, simplicity is typically essential.

Many property managers believe that the more complex the form the more professional they appear. Complexity often adds confusion and will sometimes cause the tenant to fail to perform the functions outlined within the notices. It is important that all of the regionally appropriate specifics be incorporated into any notice you generate, but it is equally important that the notices be concise and easy to understand.

Reports were discussed briefly in the descriptive narration of job functions. The compilation of concise reports is a very important factor for the property owner or management firm. As with notices, all reports should incorporate all of the necessary information in the most efficient manner possible. The record keeping duties inherent in your business are incorporated to simplify the accounting that will occur in relationship to cash flow assessments and the completion of tax returns. It is important that the necessary information be easy to locate and clearly defined.

Adequate and complete reports allow the property owner or management firm to assess the stability of a rental building or complex. Reports are also used to determine what, if any, changes must be undertaken to ensure continued profitability and to determine potential problems, which may arise in the future.

The reports generated by the property manager are used for tax records and allow for predictive analysis so that the future return of a building may be assessed and potential problems isolated before they cause financial issues.

The most common reports are outlined on the following pages. You will want to review these carefully and ensure that you are adept at the completion of these reports.

Regional variances, State Laws and Regulations and the preferred practices of your office or property owner will affect the reports you will use. The example reports are similar in content to the reports you will encounter but are included for example and educational purposes only.

Notice of Rent Increase:

Dear

This is to inform you that effective _____, the rent for the unit you now occupy at _____ will be increased by $_____ per month from $_____ to $_____ per month, payable on the _____ day of each month.

All other terms and conditions of your rental lease agreement continue to remain in effect.

Thank you for your cooperation.

Sincerely,

RECEIPT FOR MONIES OWED

Date: _____

To: _____

RE: Unit # _____

The Owner hereby accepts payment in the amount of $ _____ for the following:

Rent from _____ to _____ $ _____

Late Fee $ _____

NSF Check Fee $ _____

Security Deposit $ _____

Other _____ $ _____

Other _____ $ _____

Other _____ $ _____

TOTAL $ _____

ALL CHECKS MUST BE MADE OUT TO:

_____   _____

OWNER   TENANT

Rental Activity Report

Building: _____ 30-day expiration _____

Prepared by: _____ 60-day expiration _____

Week ending: _____ 90-day expiration _____

Occupancy: _____ Vacancy _____ Available Units _____

	Walk In	Calls	Deposits	Cancelled	Leases	Move Out	Move In
Monday	_____	_____	_____	_____	_____	_____	_____
Tuesday	_____	_____	_____	_____	_____	_____	_____
Wednesday	_____	_____	_____	_____	_____	_____	_____
Thursday	_____	_____	_____	_____	_____	_____	_____
Friday	_____	_____	_____	_____	_____	_____	_____
Saturday	_____	_____	_____	_____	_____	_____	_____

Prospect Types

Marrieds_____

Family Groups _____

Empty Nester_____

Singles_____

Non-married_____

Other_____

Other_____

Media Source

Newspaper_____

Newspaper_____

Radio_____

Signs_____

Direct Mail_____

Referral_____

Other_____

Activity Notes

New Leases:

1 Year _____ 6 Months _____ Month to Month _____ Other _____

Rental Activity Notes:

_____

_____

_____

_____

_____

MONTHLY COLLECTION REPORT

Report for the property located at: _____

Report compiled by: _____

For the month of _____

Unit #	Amount	Date	Check(P)/ Cashiers(C)	Comments
1 _____	_____	_____	_____	_____
2 _____	_____	_____	_____	_____
3 _____	_____	_____	_____	_____
4 _____	_____	_____	_____	_____
5 _____	_____	_____	_____	_____
6 _____	_____	_____	_____	_____
7 _____	_____	_____	_____	_____
8 _____	_____	_____	_____	_____
9 _____	_____	_____	_____	_____

TOTAL   _____

BY: _____ DATE: _____

Intent to Access

Be advised that _____ the property manager of your rental unit requires access on _____, at _____ am/pm. As stipulated in your lease agreement, this is to be considered your formal notice of our intent to enter your unit. If you wish to be present during the access, you are welcome to do so. If you would like to attempt to arrange a more convenient time for the access, please contact our offices by calling _____ during our posted business hours. In the event you are unavailable at the designated time for access, _____, _____ will be present.

Date: _____

Notice Posted By: _____

Property Vacate Report

Unit # _____ Unit Address: _____
Tenant's Name: _____
Forwarding Address: _____
_____
_____
Phone #: _____ Date Vacated:_____ Date of Notice: _____

DAMAGES   COST

_____
_____
_____
_____
_____
_____
_____

UNPAID AMOUNTS
  Rent _____
  Late Fees _____
  Other _____
  _____
  _____
  TOTAL _____

Reason for move:
_____
_____
_____

Comments:
_____
_____

Prepared by: _____
Date_____

LOAN PAYMENT WORKSHEET

Date	Payment	Impounds Insurance Taxes	Payment Analysis Interest	Principal
____	_____	_____	_____	_____
____	_____	_____	_____	_____
____	_____	_____	_____	_____
____	_____	_____	_____	_____
____	_____	_____	_____	_____
____	_____	_____	_____	_____
____	_____	_____	_____	_____
____	_____	_____	_____	_____
____	_____	_____	_____	_____
____	_____	_____	_____	_____
____	_____	_____	_____	_____
Total	_____	_____	_____	_____

Minimum Charges for Services and Turnover Costs
AS OF ___/___/___

The charges below (although they do not cover all items) are the most common charges in residence turnover or accidental damage done by a resident.

It is the desire of management that no charges will have to be made to any resident. If the property requires additional cleaning, repairs or replacement, we want you to be aware of the costs.

Please keep in mind these are minimum charges, actual charges may be higher.

ITEM	Minimum Charges	ITEM	Minimum Charges
Carpet cleaning per room	$95.00	Kitchen/bath drain stopper	$8.00
Carpet repair	$50.00	Replace patio door screen	30.00
Replace wall to wall carpet (per room)	$500.00	Replace window screen	$15.00
Damage to resilient flooring (cost to replace)	$30.00	General cleaning (Washing Windows, Sinks, Toilets, Mirrors, Cabinets, Refrigerator, Stove)	$185.00
Labor cost for painting - per room	$150.00	Chip on sink or tub (each)	$10.00
Painting (1 bedroom)	250.00	Chip on kitchen appliances	$10.00
Paint touch up	$20.00	Damage to ceramic tile	$30.00
Paint per gallon-turnover	$20.00	Damage to counter top	$30.00
Drywall touch up	$10.00	Damage to cabinets	$25.00
Nail holes per hole	$1.00	Cleaning range	$25.00
Trash removal-exterior or interior	$35.00	Turnover hourly work per hour	$25.00
Entrance key not returned each	$50.00	Replace storm window frame	30.00
Mailbox key not returned	25.00	Replace smoke alarm	$25.00

each			
Replace storm door with closer	110.00	Replace smoke alarm battery	$3.50
Replace interior door	$100.00	Replace refrigerator vegetable tray	$35.00
Replace exterior door	$175.00	Replace butter dish	$5.00
Damage to woodwork	$25.00	Replace ice cube tray	$2.00
Replace light bulbs each	$2.00	Replace ice caddies	$8.00
Repair or replace light fixture	$35.00	Replace broiler pan	$30.00
Replace door stop	$2.00	Replace oven rack	$20.00
Replace traverse rod or mini blind	$25.00	Replace appliance knob or dial	$15.00
Replace or repair security locks	$45.00	Replace dishwasher utensil basket	$30.00
Replace medicine cabinet	$75.00	Broken or cracked window glass	$45.00
Replace medicine cabinet shelf	$15.00	Replace outlet or light switch plate	$2.00
Replace wall mirror	$100.00	Repair-replace toilet parts	$25.00
Replace chrome or ceramic towel bars	$25.00	Replace toilet	$150.00
Replace soap dish	$15.00	Remove foreign object from disposal	$35.00
Replace powder room mirror	$50.00	Clean out toilet, sink or street drain line	$95.00

Signing your names below shows that you have read the above and you are in complete agreement with these charges and understand this notice.

Name _____Date_____
Name _____Date_____

Year End Analysis

Expense Summary 20_____

Expense	Total	Ledger Yes/No	Receipt Yes/No
Advertising			
Auto and Travel			
Cleaning			
Insurance			
Legal Fees			
Maintenance			
Mortgage Payment Interest			
Mortgage Payment Principal			
Professional Fees			
Repairs			
Supplies			
Taxes			
Utilities			

NOTICE OF ADDITIONAL AMOUNTS OWED

Date: _____

To: _____
_____
_____
_____

RE: Unit # _____

Listed below are the damages and charges incurred by us upon your vacating the apartment unit known as: _____

DAMAGES   COST

_____
_____
_____
_____
_____
_____
_____
_____
_____
_____

UNPAID AMOUNTS
Rent _____
Late Fees _____
Other_____
Other _____
Other _____

TOTAL COSTS $_____
SECURITY DEPOSIT $_____
AMOUNT STILL OWED. $_____
As detailed above, please remit $ _____ to us promptly.

MONTHLY VACANCY REPORT

Property Address: _____

Compiled by: _____

For Month Ending _____

UNIT	DATE VACATED	DATE AVAILABLE (*)	STATUS/COMMENTS
____	_____	_____	_____
____	_____	_____	_____
____	_____	_____	_____
____	_____	_____	_____
____	_____	_____	_____
____	_____	_____	_____
____	_____	_____	_____
____	_____	_____	_____
____	_____	_____	_____
____	_____	_____	_____
____	_____	_____	_____

By: _____

Date: _____

NOTICE OF LATE FEE OWED

Date: _____

To: _____

RE: Unit # _____

We received your rent payment in the amount of $_____ on _____. Thank you.

If you recall from the rent agreement, a late payment fee is assessed for payment received after the first of the month. Therefore, we still need $_____ from you, calculated as follows:

Rent Due $ _____
Late Fee $ _____
Other _____ $ _____
Other _____ $ _____

Sub-Total of all charges $ _____

Payment Received   ($ _____)

TOTAL amount still due $ _____

Please make the check payable to _____ and mail it to the address shown below. If you have any questions, please call _____.

Sincerely,

NOTICE OF NSF CHECK CHARGE AND LATE FEE OWED

Date: _____

To: _____

RE: Unit # _____

Although we received your rent payment, the bank because of non-sufficient funds in your bank account returned your check. If you recall from the rent agreement, we must receive all rent payments on the first of every month. A late payment fee will be assessed for rent payments received after the first of every month. In addition, a non-sufficient funds service charge will be assessed for returned checks.

Because your check was marked non-sufficient funds, you must immediately pay by CASHIER'S CHECK OR MONEY ORDER. We cannot accept a personal check. Therefore, we still need $_____ from you, calculated as follows:

Rent Due	$ _____
Late Fee	$ _____
NSF Service Charge	$ _____
Other _____	$ _____
Other _____	$ _____
TOTAL	$ _____

Please make the check payable to _____ and mail it to the address shown below. If you have any questions, please call _____.

Sincerely,

NOTICE TO PAY OR QUIT TENANCY

Date: _____

To: _____

RE: Unit # _____

You are notified that you owe the amount of $_____ calculated as follows:

Rent	$_____
Late Fee	$_____
Other Charges _____	$_____
Other Charges _____	$_____
Other Charges _____	$_____
TOTAL	$ _____

You must pay this amount in cash, money order or certified check. A personal check will not be accepted.

If you fail to pay within 3 DAYS of when you receive this notice, your tenancy is terminated and you must move.

If you do not move, a lawsuit will be filed to evict you.

If you make the required payment within 3 days, you may remain in the apartment unit and no further action will be taken.

_____
Authorized Agent

The undersigned received this notice on the _____ day of _____, 20____ at _____am/pm.

_____
(Tenant)

NOTICE TO CURE VIOLATION OF AGREEMENT

Date: _____

To: _____

RE: Unit # _____

You are notified that you have violated your agreement with us in the following manner:

_____
_____
_____
_____
_____

If you fail to remedy this violation within 3 DAYS of when you receive this notice, your tenancy is terminated and you must move.

If you do not move, a lawsuit will be filed to evict you. If you remedy this violation within 3 days, you remain in the apartment unit and no further action will be taken.

_____

The undersigned received this notice on the _____ day of
_____, 20____ at _____am/pm.

_____
(Tenant)

NOTICE THAT EVICTION WILL BE FILED IN COURT

Date: _____

To: _____

RE: Unit # _____

It has come to my attention that you have failed to comply with the terms of your agreement with us dated _____, 20____.

I understand that you have been given a 3-day notice in accordance with state and local laws and have failed to move.

Therefore, I have instructed the property manager not to accept any payment from you. All amounts you still owe will be offset against your security deposit or collected in a legal action.

If you have not moved out of the apartment by _____, 20_____, I will file suit the next day.

I will also obtain an injunction forcing your removal, with the aid of the police.

The lawsuit will be for the amount owed under the agreement, the costs of filing suit, attorney's fees and enforcement. I plan to collect these amounts from you.

When you are evicted, I also plan to inform credit reporting and other agencies of this action.

This position is not negotiable.

_____

Whenever possible the investor will wish to avoid an eviction proceeding. Evictions often create a situation in which neither party wins. It is often desirable for the owner of the property to meet with the tenant and attempt to negotiate an equitable agreement that benefits both parties.

When an eviction process is taken through the courts, the property owner typically receives access to their property and a judgment for monies owed by the tenant. This judgment is often difficult to collect.

It will be the owner's responsibility to ensure the judgment is placed on the tenant's credit report and any collection activity that occurs because of the judgment will be the duty of the investor.

Some investors find that they can create a win-win situation out of a potential eviction process through open discussion with the tenant. At times, a particular situation exists that is causing the financial strain on the tenant. A previously excellent performance on the part of the tenant may be adequate cause for the property owner to choose to work with the tenant on payments until they are able to regain their financial equilibrium and begin making payments as agreed once more. A tenant who does not choose to enter a payment arrangement may still be willing to make a financial settlement with the property owner in exchange for the property owner's agreement not to enter an eviction and subsequent judgment against the tenant. This settlement will typically not compensate the investor for the entire amount due under the lease agreement but any additional funds provided by the tenant will be considered a positive entry on the investor's cash flow analysis. Open negotiations may limit the financial hardship an eviction and subsequent vacancy can inflict upon the property owner and may allow the property owner to maintain a positive relationship with a potentially good tenant during financial hardship.

At times, an eviction process is inevitable. When the investor must proceed with the eviction process, there are certain steps they will take.

- Send a notice to the tenant as soon as the rent payment is late or another infraction outlined in the lease has occurred.

The investor or property manager should ensure that this notice is delivered via registered mail so that proper practices can be proven in the future.

- File a landlord/tenant complaint with the magistrate or other court of jurisdiction.

  Each jurisdiction will have a specific waiting period in which the tenant has the opportunity to respond to the complaint. A standard is 30 days. Following this waiting period, the courts will issue an order of eviction. If the tenant appeals the eviction during their allocated time, the tenant may escrow any rent payments due to the property owner until the courts have issued a ruling.

- If an eviction is granted, the property owner may then file a personal judgment against the tenant. The property owner will take the transcript from the magistrate hearing to the prothonotory's office in their county to file the judgment.

- The property owner will then need to submit the judgment to the credit reporting agencies to have the judgment entered into the tenant's credit record. Additional collection activity may then be taken.

APPENDIX
GLOSSARY OF TERMS

Addendum
A document that becomes part of another document including the lease agreement. Addenda are often used to alter the terms or conditions of a lease.

Adjusted Basis
The value of a property for tax purposes. The calculation will consist of the property purchase price plus improvements made, closing costs paid less depreciation.

After-tax Cash Flow
The calculations of cash flow incorporating both incomes received and expenses paid out.

Amenities
Intangible qualities of a property that assist in generating a pleasant, comfortable environment that leads to tenant satisfaction. These items include but are not limited to items that create consumer interest or generate appeal. These amenities are considered a selling point or benefit.

Annual
A consecutive 12-month period

Apartment
A dwelling unit that is used for the residence of one or more individuals

Appreciation
An increase in value

Assessments
The value given to a property for the purpose of taxation

Budget
A formal estimate of the probable cost of operations in the future.

Capital Gains
The difference between the cost value and the selling price of a piece of real estate. Capital gains can be accounted on items other than real estate. Capital gains figures are used in tax calculations.

Cash Flow
The net cash remaining after all operating and fixed expenses are paid. The expenses do not include tax and depreciation costs.

Chattel
Personal Property

Commission
Compensation paid to a lender or real estate agent in return for performance of a service in a transaction. Commissions are typically paid as a percentage of total sales prices or financed amount.

Common Area
The portion of an investment property used by all individuals

Depreciation
A deduction in value from the highest level caused by deterioration or obsolescence of a piece of real estate

Depreciation Future
The estimate of the loss as it is likely to occur in the future.

Effective Gross Income
The possible gross income attributable to a particular property or unit after the

allowance for vacancy loss and collection losses is accounted.

Economic Rent
The expected rent justified by the demand in a particular region.

Equity
Fair market value of a property or land minus all liens and encumbrances

Escalation Clause
An agreement clause that allows for the increase in rental figures to compensate for increase in costs such as taxes, business conditions, utility costs or other items.

Fair Market Rent
The amount of rental money a unit may command in the present market.

Feasibility Study
The application of analytical study to a proposed project or purchase.

Future Depreciation
The loss in value that will occur in the future

Gross Lease
A lease under which the property owner pays all expenses.

Gross Operating Income
The incomes from a property before the applicable expenses are calculated.

Leasehold Interest
The interest or rights given to a tenant through the implementation of a lease.

Lessee
Person who rents a property from another Tenant

Lessor
Person who rents a property to another Landlord, owner, investor

Leverage
A term applied to the investment benefit created by using borrowed funds to purchase income-producing property. The difference between the investments earned yield and the cost of the borrowed funds.

Liquidity
The availability of cash in a particular investment

Market Rent
The average rent that can be obtained from a particular unit based on economic and regional conditions that affect the rent received from other, similar units.

Negative Cash Flow
A scenario in which more money is paid out on a monthly basis than is received from an investment.

Net Lease
A lease under which the tenant pays all expenses.

Net Operating Income
The incomes of a property after all income and expenses have been calculated.

Obsolescence
A loss in value because of a property being functionally deficient or out of date

Occupancy Rate
The calculation of the time that a unit is occupied versus the time the unit is

vacant. This rate is expressed as a percentage and may be reflected as a vacancy rate.

Operating Expense
Expense incurred because of the operation and maintenance of a property.

Operating Ratio
The comparison in percentage between the stabilized operating expense and the effective gross income of a property

Past Depreciation
Depreciation that has occurred in the past.

Percentage Lease
A lease that bases the rental charges on a percentage of the volume of business done on the premises.

Personal Property
Movable items that are not permanently affixed to real estate and are considered owned separately from the real property.

Physical Depreciation
The loss in value occurring from wear and tear and deterioration of a property that is not repaired

Positive Cash Flow
A scenario in which the income received from a unit exceeds the cash expenses of the investment on a monthly basis.

Recovery Period
The period allocated for the depreciation of an investment real estate property.

Rehabilitation
Restoration of a property to its former condition

Remodeling
The altering of a property that alters the former layout, style, or function

Renovation
The collective term used to describe any alterations to a property including repair rehabilitation and remodeling.

Reserve
An amount of money held aside against expected expense.

Sub Lease
The assignment of a lease by the tenant to another individual.

Vacancy Rate
The calculation of the time that a unit is vacant versus the time the unit is occupied. This rate is expressed as a percentage and may be reflected as an occupancy rate.

Zoning
The allowed use of a piece of real property set by the established governmental codes and ordinances.

www.ingramcontent.com/pod-product-compliance
Lightning Source LLC
Chambersburg PA
CBHW080811280326
41926CB00091B/4264